Give Me The Children

Give Me The CHILDREN

How A Christian Woman Saved a Jewish Family During the Holocaust

Pola Arbiser

Authors Choice Press
New York   Bloomington

Give Me The Children
How A Christian Woman Saved a Jewish Family During the Holocaust

Authors Choice Press
an imprint of iUniverse, Inc.

iUniverse books may be ordered through booksellers or by contacting:

iUniverse
1663 Liberty Drive
Bloomington, IN 47403
www.iuniverse.com
1-800-Authors (1-800-288-4677)

ISBN: 978-1-4502-5180-8 (sc)

Printed in the United States of America

iUniverse rev. date: 08/04/2010

TABLE OF CONTENTS

In memory of Franciszka Sobkowa who was honored as a
Righteous Gentile in 1999 for her rescue of Pola, Irene,
and Sara Bienstock during the war.
Thank you Frania for
your unconditional love and life.

A few years ago an article appeared in our local newspaper, the *Atlanta Journal-Constitution*, stating that CNN was planning to introduce a program about Holocaust survivors. The person who would introduce the program would be an American Jew who was chosen because he "looked like a Holocaust survivor." I was appalled that CNN believed there was such a thing as a "typical" Holocaust survivor. Didn't Hilter similarly depict the "typical Jew" as a sinister-looking, dark, ugly, hook-nosed creature? I wrote a letter to the newspaper in which I stated that I, a Holocaust survivor, did not resemble this man at all and neither did my survivor friends. Apparently as a result of my letter CNN dropped the idea of using a "typical" Holocaust survivor.

A few days later, I received a call from a man named Robert Callner, who worked for CNN. Mr. Callner had read my letter to the newspaper and was impressed with the story of Frania Sobkowa's selfless rescue of my family during the war. He asked if he could come to our house and meet me and my family. I agreed and a few days later a pleasant-looking young man with a guitar appeared on our doorstep.

He told me that he had composed a song in honor of Frania called *Silent Hero.* He played and sang it for us. We were very touched by his kindness. The text of that song follows:

1

SILENT HERO
[Dedicated to Franciska Sobkowa)
Words and Music by Bob Callner

They went walking on Sundays
In the warm sun to Monday's hope
They could not see it come

In a small town in Poland
Before the War had stolen lives
There was laughter and fun.

Frania did the only thing she could do
A Silent Hero carried on
She could not save her nation from the coming doom
But she gave the World to a few

The Germans would have shot her
And the children that she hid from them
She kept up the silent fight

Every breathe of life she heard
Was a song she sang word for word
To lead them to the light.

Frania did the only thing she could do
A Silent Hero carried on
She could not save her nation from the coming doom
But she gave the World to a few

Day to day
We pray for dark skies
Night to night
We fight for sunrise

Frania did the only thing she could do
A Silent Hero carries on
She could not save her nation from the coming doom
But she gave the World to a few
That's all I'd hope to ever do
Just to give the World to a few.

By Pola Arbiser during her time in hiding

In shackles of hard oppression
I am sitting and thinking of a beautiful world
And about my horrible, inhuman fate.
I am sitting and waiting!
    I am sitting and thinking that, after all,
    Someday I will emerge from this hell.
    That there still are people in this God's world
    I am sitting and thinking that I will get out of here yet!
I am sitting! Flickering inside me there is still hope
That I will be watching this beautiful world,
That a magician's hand will change all this,
And we will be like brothers to each other.
    I am sitting and thinking and my thoughts are flowing,
    Flowing like a big wave, like a rapid river.
    Over these waves my thoughts will quickly spread
    And my heart is still crying and lamenting.
And when I lose all strength because of crying,
My heart plucks up courage anew.
"Imp Scoffer" tells me new tales,
I still believe in good spirit; I am sitting and waiting!
    "Sylwester Ostrozny" (a fictional character's name)

INTRODUCTION

For some time, my sister Pola has been talking about writing a book about Frania Sobkowa, the woman who saved our lives during World War II. I did not embrace the idea with great enthusiasm. I felt that many books have been written on the subject—each different, each one a miracle—and that enough was enough. Finally, Pola convinced me that it was important to celebrate the life of Frania. As the younger sister who had always ardently admired my older sibling—and who in my eyes could do no wrong—I promised to cooperate.

For many years I had difficulty talking about my wartime experiences. I did however dream about them a lot—about hiding, running, being pursued by the Germans, and running out of hiding places. It is only recently that I started talking and writing short stories, many of which draw on my childhood experiences. As I did so I dreamt less and less often—perhaps my writing and talking has replaced the dreams.

My sister was ardent about writing about Frania, the unusual young Polish woman who was our savior. She told me that on the cover of the book she wanted to put a picture of Frania with her and my older brother. My family lost everything during the war, and this photo was one of the few pictures that survived probably because it had adorned the wall of Frania's modest apartment. The picture shows a very young Frania, who was at the time the housekeeper and nanny in my parent's home, and my sister and brother who were three and five years old, respectively. I am not in the picture—most likely I was a home in my crib.

I was a chubby, clumsy child who wore glasses and was given to seriousness and precocity. I did not feel that I was as beautiful as my older sister, Pola, who was tall and long-legged with beautiful dark eyes and long thick braids. She was elegant and self-assured—the kind of child you like to show off. But it never really bothered me. I always adored my sister and constantly bragged about her. When I started school my sentences always started with: "My sister Pola ..." It was a standing joke among my friends.

I grew up in a small town in Poland called Drohobycz that is today in the Ukraine. Drohobycz was small but it had a cosmopolitan flavor. It was known for its oil wells and many people became rich almost overnight. The unexpected riches caused some extravagant escapades: men suddenly got rid of their old wives and married younger and prettier women. Old married women took handsome boyfriends. Many people traveled abroad.

However, at the same time there was a lot of poverty. When I was six or seven years old, the mother of a girlfriend with whom I was playing, called me in, took her wedding ring off and asked me to take it home to my mother as collateral for a five *zloty* loan (at the time about one dollar). Because I was young I did not understand how poor they were; it took many years for me to understand it.

My father, Israel Bienstock, was a successful businessman. He was educated, intelligent, handsome, and well-traveled. He had a facility for languages and was extremely self-assured. He liked to show off and enjoyed attention. My mother, Sara, was tall, beautiful, and elegant. Unlike my father, however, my mother was quiet, modest, did not gossip, had very few friends, and was very charitable-but in an anonymous way.

At a very early age I learned from her the importance of charity. In Drohobycz, the winters could be severe and many families could not afford warm clothing for their children. The teachers at my school appealed to parents to send warm coats, sweaters, and shoes for the needy children. The clothes were distributed to the student in front of the class—an act I found to be well-intentioned but cruel. My mother, on the other hand, sent a big bag of clothes to school with Frania, and instructed her to unobtrusively call a needy child into the bathroom during recess so nobody would see the transfer. I often saw my friends wearing my dresses and coats and would pretend I did not notice.

I was always surrounded by a loving family, of which Frania was considered a member. I also had many uncles, aunts, and cousins, few of whom survived the war.

That all changed when the war started in September 1939. Our father joined the Polish army for a short while, during which time Drohobycz was taken over the by Russians, who promptly confiscated his store and merchandise, our house, and all our money. We were told to leave town by the Russians as our family represented an undesirable capitalist element and we went to live with my mother's sister in a nearby town. By that time my older brother, Ludwik, had died of pneumonia and my parents—especially my mother—were devastated. My mother never really recovered from his loss. But my sister and I learned fast not to show our grief that deepened even more when our father was captured and taken away by the Germans.

The Germans occupied Drohobycz in June 1941. My family survived the first deadly pogrom that took place under German domination during which the Germans permitted our non-Jewish neighbors to do what they wanted without interference. And they did. Within twenty-four hours many people with whom we had been friendly before the war, robbed, maimed, and murdered their Jewish neighbors. Later, I wrote a story entitled "Grand Dame" about one of these people.

Shortly before the outbreak of the war, Frania married. Frania was a nice-looking, blond-haired, short woman with blue eyes and a small upturned nose.She was pleasant and jolly, quick with a joke or a laugh. Frania had not lacked suitors (she was rather popular actually) as she had a good steady job and substantial savings. The marriage took some convincing on my mother's part as Frania felt we were her children and she had no desire to leave. However, my mother convinced her that eventually we would grow up and she would be lonely. The wedding was a simple modest affair with members of her family and a few friends.

After Frania's marriage, her sister, Marysia, took over her position as nursemaid and housekeeper and Frania visited every day to make sure everything was in order. Regrettably, Frania's marriage was short-lived as her husband was conscripted into the Russian army and he did not return from the front.

At first, when the Germans occupied Drohobycz after two years of Russian rule, my parents were
quite relieved. My father knew Germany and the
Germans, as he had often traveled there on business, and considered them to be cultured and civi-
lized as opposed to the 'barbaric' Russians. Thus,
the first pogrom that was instigated by our Polish
neighbors but condoned by the Germans, shook our
entire family up badly.Luckily, we found temporary
shelter in the attic of a female acquaintance—for
which my parents paid the woman handsomely.

After a few days when the violence died down we
returned to our home in Drohobycz. It was empty
having been abandoned by the Russians who had
lived there for two years. But the Germans began
to concentrate the Jews into one area and shortly
thereafter three other Jewish families moved in
with us. Germans and Ukrainians entered our home
at will and took anything they pleased away with
them. Jewish people were rounded up on the streets
and forced into menial labor.

Our family survived thanks to our father's re-
sourcefulness, to luck, and, of course, to Frania.

In December 1942 there was a month-long *Aktion* during which the Germans rounded up children and old people, whom they took to the forest and shot. My beautiful mother aged fast during this time—her hair turned white, although she was only in her early forties.

My father found a place for us to live in the cellar of the building where he worked. Pola, who was tall for her age also secured a job after getting the necessary documents. After a few weeks in these cruel conditions, my mother was injured by a German bullet and my father, sister, and I were arrested and taken to Gestapo headquarters. Again a miracle occurred. On a whim, the Gestapo chief let us go.

It was in November 1942 that a well-known writer and painter, Bruno Schulz, was murdered in the streets of Drohobycz by the Germans. I remember clearly when my father told us: "Today they killed on the street Bruno Schulz." Shortly after this episode, Frania came to the ghetto and took me away with her to her small apartment. Frania worked for a Gestapo man as a cook and left the house very early each morning and returned late every evening. I had to remain totally quiet and not move while she was gone. I was very lonely and frightened while Frania was at work but it was a time when children matured fast. A few months later I was joined by my mother. My father and my sister, Pola, had escaped the liquidation of the ghetto at the very last minute. Frania's apartment was very small—one room and a small kitchen—and there was no room for my father. He hid in the woods where he was later captured and taken off to the first of six concentration camps.

Frania shared with us what little food she had—somehow she stretched food for only one person into nourishment for four. In the main room of the apartment was a door that led to another couple's apartment. The door was covered by a piece of furniture. While Frania was at work, we were not allowed to move. Pola and I whispered to each other under the bed, telling each other stories. We had no books, no newspapers, and no radio. But worst of all we were deadly scared for ourselves and Frania, as well as worried about our father's fate. Often Frania brought home terrible stories about Jewish people and their would-be rescuers, who, when they were caught, were publicly killed together in the middle of town, so that anyone considering doing the same knew what fate awaited them.

Under those conditions, my sister, my mother and I spent two-and-one-half years. As a result, I developed a special relationship with my sister—she was my only friend and mentor for a long time. Frania never complained even though she must have been frightened as well. I was too young at the time to realize what a risk she was taking. Recently, someone who heard my story, told me that Frania had been sent to us from heaven. It had never occurred to me before but now I realize it was true. So, this book is for my sister, Pola, but most of all for Frania who made it possible for me to write this today.

Irene Frisch

Frania after the war

Frania in the park with Ludwik and Pola circa 1934.

Chapter 1
Incidental Meeting

The incidental meeting that occurred between my mother and Frania before I was born secured our family's survival during World War II. Incidental unforeseen events often change the history of nations and people. One such event happened to my family.

One day my mother, Sara, was pushing my brother, Ludwik, in a stroller on the streets of Drohobycz when she was stopped by two young girls. The meeting happened a few years before myself and Irene, my younger sister, were born. The two girls lived on a farm outside the city and had come into the city for an eye examination. Frania, the younger of the two girls, stopped my mother and began to play with my brother, Ludwik, with whom she fell instantly in love. My mother asked if she would like to come home with her and take care of my brother. Frania agreed even though her sister urged her to return home.

My father was very upset when Frania first appeared in our home as she was a total stranger. My parents decided to check her out. They left my brother in her care and said they were leaving to visit a friend. Instead, they sneaked around the back of the one-story house and observed Frania through the window, who was singing and rocking my brother. They decided she would work out. As the years went on, Frania took over complete responsibility for the household.

Frania's devotion to us knew no boundaries. She would not allow anyone to harm us and she saw in us only positive traits. From 1942 to 1945, Frania hid my mother, myself, and my sister in her small apartment even though aiding Jews was punishable by death. She shared everything with us including every scrap of food. But what Frania gave us was far more than just food or housing—she gave us life.

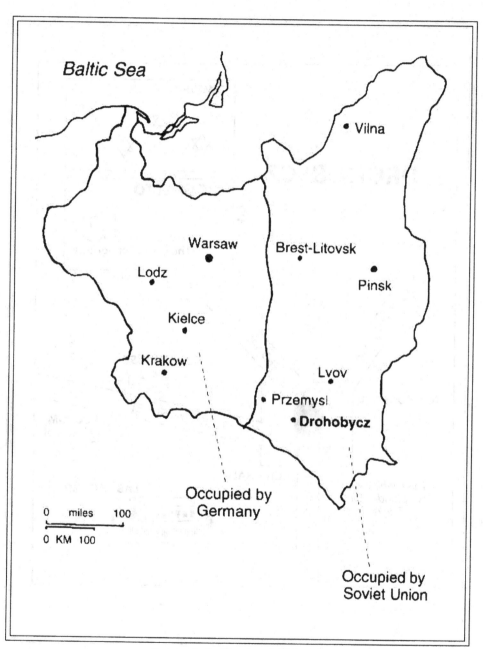

Baltic Sea

Vilna

Warsaw

Brest-Litovsk

Lodz

Pinsk

Kielce

Krakow

Lvov

Przemysl

Drohobycz

Occupied by
Germany

0 miles 100

0 KM 100

Occupied by
Soviet Union

Map of Poland, 1939-40

19

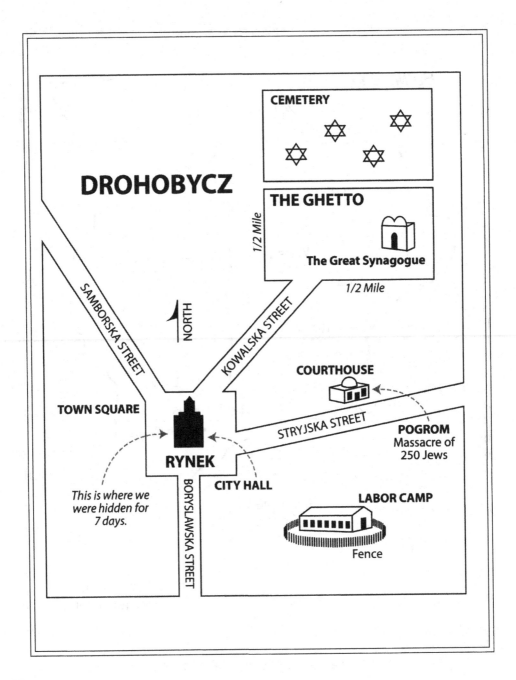

DROHOBYCZ

CEMETERY

THE GHETTO

The Great Synagogue

1/2 Mile

1/2 Mile

NORTH

SAMBORSKA STREET

KOWALSKA STREET

COURTHOUSE

TOWN SQUARE

STRYJSKA STREET

POGROM
Massacre of
250 Jews

RYNEK

This is where we
were hidden for
7 days.

BORYSLAWSKA STREET

CITY HALL

LABOR CAMP

Fence

Chapter 2:
The History of Drohobycz

Drohobycz was a city in eastern Poland and Jews have lived there since the fifteenth century. On the eve of World War II, the Jewish community numbered some 7,000. In September 1939 when Germany invaded Poland, Drohobycz fell briefly into German hands. In that short time, the Germans gave the non-Jewish population a free hand to "take care" of the Jews. Many of them eagerly used this permission to kill hundreds of Jews and rob them of their possessions. Shortly thereafter, Drohobycz came into Russian hands due to an agreement between Hitler and Stalin.

Following the German invasion of Russia in June 1941, the Germans again occupied Drohobycz. Groups of young Jews tried to flee from Drohobycz to the East. Many were killed in the attempt, either during German air attacks or at the hands of Ukrainian nationalists who were active in the area.

German forces entered the city on June 30, 1941 and the next day another pogrom took place. It lasted for three days and over its course Ukrainian and Wehrmacht soldiers murdered over 300 Jews.

In July 1941, various measures against the Jews were introduced. Jews were seized at random and made to perform forced labor. The movement of Jews in the main streets was restricted. Many Jews were compelled to vacate their apartments so that German officers could move in. Jews were banned from the city market and they had to wear on their right-hand sleeve a white band with the Star of David.

The *Judenrat* (Jewish council) which was set up in July sought to reach an agreement with the German authorities regarding forced labor by Jews. In order to avoid the random seizures it undertook to supply fixed quotas of laborers. This effort, however, met with only limited success. The *Judenrat* also opened soup kitchens that dispensed meals to the needy.

In September and October of 1941, several dozen Jewish intellectuals were arrested and all trace of them was lost. Later, it became known that they had been tortured and then murdered in the forest of Bronica near the city. On November 30, another 300 Jews were murdered in the same place. That winter many Jews died of starvation and typhus. In the spring of 1942, the *Judenrat* set up workshops to create employment for the Jewish population in the hope that this would save them from being sent to the work camps that had been set up nearby, where harsh conditions caused the death of many of the inmates. Hundreds of the city's Jews were also employed in local oil refineries and in the processing of oil products.

At the end of March 1942, an *Aktion* took place that resulted in 2,000 Jews being sent to their deaths in the Belzec extermination camp. A second large *Aktion* was launched on August 8 and lasted until August 17, 1942. Selections were made at the various assembly points and only workers with

An *Aktion* in Drohobycz

employment cards with essential jobs in the oil industry were exempt.

Germans, Poles, and Ukrainian collaborators hunted down Jews in hiding and anyone they found was murdered. They sent their children to search out the hidden Jews for which the Germans paid 500 *zlotys* per head—the cost of a loaf of bread. More than 600 Jews were killed in the city courtyards and alleys and over 2,500 were deported to Belzec. My mother's aunt, Yentl, was taken at this time.

An *Aktion* in Drobobycz

At the beginning of October 1942, a ghetto was established in Drohobycz in which thousands of Jews were confined, among them the remnants of Jewish communities in the vicinity. Another *Aktion* took place on October 23 and 24 in

which 2,300 Jews were sent to Belzec and 300 patients in the Jewish hospital were killed. Still
another *Aktion* was launched in November and went
on uninterrupted for an entire month. Ten days
after it started, 1,000 Jews were taken to Belzec
by train and few days later several hundreds more.
Hundreds of others were killed in the ghetto.

At the end of 1942 and in the beginning of 1943,
the Jews who worked in the oil industry were put
in separate work camps. On February 15, 1943 four
hundred fifty Jews were taken out of the ghetto to
Bronica forest where they were murdered. The liquidation of the ghetto began on May 21 and was
completed by June 10. At the same time the *Judenrat*
ceased to function. Many of the ghetto houses
were set on fire in order to force out any Jews who
had hidden inside. The last Jews found in the
ghetto, including my aunt and cousin, were put on
trucks and taken to Bronica forest, where they
were killed and buried in pits.

The destruction of the ghetto was followed by the
murder of the Jews in the work camps, with only
the most essential of the workers left alive.
Following the Soviet advance in April 1944 these

workers were sent west to the Plaszow labor camp. When the Soviet army entered Drohobcyz in 1945, only a few Jewish survivors emerged from their hiding places.[1]

[1] Most of the factual information in this chapter came from the "Drohobycz" entry in the *Holocaust Encyclopedia*.

Chapter 3
Drohobycz During My Childhood

When I was born in Drohobycz, the city belonged to
Poland. Drohobycz had a total population of 35,000
persons and was composed of three ethnic groups:
Poles, Ukrainians, and Jews. Jews comprised a serious portion of the population or about 7,000 people.
The city was also very well known because of the oil
fields that surrounded it. Many people lived a very
good life because of the oil.

Of course, as in many other small towns, there were
poor people in Drohobycz. The poorer Jews lived in a
part of the town called 'Lany' that was close to the
Jewish cemetery. These Jews were not well educated
and were poorly dressed. Even in our neighborhood,
I had a friend whose family lived in one room with a
dirt floor and most of the time they were hungry.

It was difficult for these poor Jewish people to
enter the social and economic mainstream but even

wealthy, educated Jews found it hard to enter the professions such as law and medicine because of the quota system in the universities which limited the number of Jews who could attain a higher education.

One exception was the Jewish painter Lilian, who was born in Drohobycz to a very poor family. Often, when he was hungry he came to my grandmother's home and asked for food, in return for which he drew her portrait in coal on the wall of the kitchen. Later, Lilian left Poland for Germany where he became very well known in the German art community at the end of the nineteenth century.

Another famous citizen of Drohobycz was the Jewish painter and writer, Bruno Schulz (1892-1942). He was considered to be "Poland's Kafka" and wrote several books including *Cinnamon Shops* (known in the United states as *Street of Crododiles)* (1933) and *The Sanatorium Under the Sign of the Hourglass* (1937). His stories and paintings are dreamlike reflections on life in the modest Jewish quarter of Drohobycz, the town of his birth. On November 19, 1942, he was shot to death on the streets of his home town by the Gestapo. Schulz was my drawing teacher in elementary school.

Bruno Schulz
1892-1942

Unrecognized until after World War II, Schulz is now considered the finest modern Polish-languaged prose stylist. His stories are based on the geography and people of his hometown of Drohobycz and like the town he called his writings a "labyrinth of new adventures and chapters." Before he was murdered by the Gestapo in the streets of Drohobycz in 1942 he wrote two books and a novella. Another novel, *The Messiah*, has been lost.

Schulz was also a painter. His last known work was a series of murals based on Grimm's fairy tales, painted under duress, for the nursery walls of a Gestapo officer's son. Schulz was working on them when he was shot to death on November 19, 1942 in the street by a Gestapo man who held a grudge against his employer. The murals were discovered by the then resident of the apartment in late 2000. Yad Vashem acquired them and took them to Israel, which started a bitter international debate, yet to be resolved, over their legal ownership.

Drohobycz had its share of characters. Moyshe Luzer, was a matchmaker. He had a complete grasp of the tricks of matchmaking. If he entered a young man's apartment, he announced that it needed a 'woman's touch' and promptly introduced just the young woman to do that. Although he was poor he always dressed immaculately and had perfect manners. He had a sister in New York who invited him to come to the United States just a few months before World War II started.

Moyshe Luzer left Drohobycz but a few months later my mother met him on the street again. She asked him what he was doing back in Drohobycz and he told her that he had liked New York except for the traffic in the streets. He had asked his sister to talk to the mayor of New York and ask him to slow down the traffic. His sister could not, so he returned. He was among the Jews of Drohobycz that were murdered in the Holocaust.

An interesting family in our city was the family Suchestov. Mr. Suchestov was an elderly wealthy widower with grown children. He married a very beautiful young woman named Jeanette from Germany and they had one son. Jeanette became bored with life in this small city and complained to my father that the seats in her chauffeur-driven car were too hard. One day she left her husband and went to Krakow. There she met Prince Radziwil and became captivated by the idea of marrying into the Polish nobility. Prince Radziwil and Jeanette went to Monte Carlo, where Prince Radziwil left her under threat of his family that if he married her he would be excluded from his father's will.

Eventually Jeanette returned to Drohobycz and was taken back by her husband. The Polish newspaper's headlines made much of the affair. *Suchestov, Tuchestov, Mazel Tov.* ['Suchestov, good behind, and good luck.'] Jeanette survived the war by singing for the Germans in concentration camps.

The street where we lived was called Zupna Street. At the end of the street, there was a well that contained a high concentration of salt. A factory called Salina was built over the well that evaporated water from the brine and salt was the end product. The soil that surrounded Salina was so salty that beets from the surrounding fields—which are usually sweet—were salty.

My father, Israel Bienstock, was in the fur business. My mother's brother was already in the fur industry in Leipzig, Germany and after my mother and father married, my uncle introduced my father to the fur business. My father came from a well-educated family. He finished high school just before World War I began. My grandparents were afraid that my father would be drafted, so they pulled some strings and he was accepted to a military academy in Trieste, Italy.

After World War I, my father's mother passed away at age 59 with breast cancer. She was a high school teacher and taught German literature.

My father was a charming, handsome man. Eventually, he established his own fur business in Drohobycz in which he was very successful. He was able to give his family a good life and we lived in a very nice one-family house. We had a car, and sometimes two.

My father also liked fishing very much and often went to the mountains and surrounding areas to pursue his hobby. On Sunday mornings, he and his friends— usually non-Jews—came to pick him up in their cars. They blew their horns outside the house to alert my

My father, Israel Bienstock, was an avid fisherman.
Here he is in the early 1960s showing off a fish he
has caught.

father to their presence. My mother was embarrassed: "What nice Jewish man fishes?" The men spent the whole day fishing, equipped with food and drink. Later, during one of the actions, one of these men promised to help hide my sister and me, but he never came.

Pola, Ludwik and Irene swimming with a relative

During one of his fishing escapades, my father took all of us with him to the River Dniester. We set out in a convertible automobile. My father announced that at a certain point he thought that the river was shallow enough for the car to cross. He was wrong, however, and water quickly filled the car. As the water level climbed to our necks, we grew very frightened. People with horses pulled the car from the water. We children undressed and waited for both the car and our clothes to dry out before we continued.

My parents belonged to a small Orthodox *stiebel* (synagogue) where many of their friends also attended. Richly-dressed women in elegant jewelry also came to the synagogue. Once, during *Yom Kippur* services in 1938, someone threw a rock through the window of the synagogue and hit my father in the head. The resulting slash covered his face with blood.

In the years after Frania's arrival, I was born, followed by my sister, Irene, two-and-one-half years later. In Frania's eyes, we could do no wrong although we were energetic and unruly children. Once when we went to play with another child in her home, like children everywhere we turned the house upside down. The other child became frightened and started throwing up. The mother called Frania and insisted that she come and take us home. Frania got very

Pola and Irene as teenagers after the war

upset and told her: "Your child is not normal if she cannot play with my children."

In the second grade I gave a piano recital at school. I'm sure I made plenty of mistakes, but when we returned home and my mother asked how I had done, Frania praised me profusely, saying that all eyes had been only on me! My piano teacher, Miss Henia, was my mother's school friend. She never married and sustained herself by giving piano lessons to children in their homes. One day, I didn't want to practice the piano so I gave her some cherry liqueur, saying that our mother had left it for her.

Miss Henia drank the whole thing and became so tipsy she could not sit up. Frania laid her out on the sofa and when she recovered she went home. Frania never told my parents about the incident.

Frania had blond hair, blue eyes, and a very sunny disposition. At the time of the incidental meeting, Frania's last name was Badecka. Her father had passed away at an early age leaving her mother with six children.

Frania's oldest sister, Kasia, had six fingers on each hand and when she came and visited we children were fascinated by this phenomenon. Kasia married a widower who had two children.

Frania's brother, Franciszek, was a policeman and liked to drink. He used to come to our home and Frania always fed him and took care of him. Another of Frania's sisters, Hania, was very pretty with a dark complexion and dark hair. She married a Ukrainian, which was a terrible thing for the family as there was a long history of enmity between Poles and Ukrainians. He was a teacher and she lived in the country. She used to visit us as well.

Marysia, another sister, was a tall, pretty, blond girl. Eventually, she also came to work for our family. The youngest child was Joseph. When he was in the Polish army he used to visit us. One night while he was sleeping I put on his belt and bayonet. The bayonet was too long and I was too short and it dragged on the floor.

Frania's mother came every Monday from the country to the city and ate with us. She brought us a special bread that she had baked and my father always gave her five *zlotys* which before the war was a lot of money. It could sustain a family of four for one day. She often brought ears of corn as well. We roasted them on long spits in an open fire. The result was delicious.

In 1939, Frania married a quiet man named Nicola Sobkow. Frania never spent the money my parents paid her. Instead she saved it, and when she married Nicola she purchased a horse and buggy for her new husband in which he delivered beer. Frania had been married about one year when the Russians came and drafted Nicola into the army. She never saw him again. If he had not been drafted, it is very likely that Frania would not have been able to hide us. Nicola was a very nice man but I doubt that he would have been willing to risk his life for us.

Before the war, during the holidays of Christmas and New Years, Frania went home to visit her family and before she left, she prepared a package for them. My mother had an aunt who made a very large *challah* with raisins. The *challah* filled a big box a meter in length. Frania also took things to drink and scarves for each of her sisters and mother, which my mother bought for them. We always took Frania to the train for her journey home.

Before I started elementary school, Frania had an argument with my mother and she left our home. My brother, Ludwik, was very upset that Frania was leaving and he hid her shoes. Nevertheless, Frania went to work for a wealthy non-Jewish family. Frania's new employers lived in a villa with thirteen rooms and had two children older than me. Every week Frania called my mother and told her, "Send me the children on Sunday."

Frania's new employer was not pleased when Frania took us to her room where she gave us chocolate and

My brother, Ludwik Bienstock, at age 5 or 6

candies and talked with us about the activities of the week. Frania stayed with this new family for only a few months, and soon returned to our family because, she said, she missed the children too much.

On Sundays, Frania went to Mass and we cried when she left. One day my brother, Ludwik, again stole her shoes so she could not go to church. Finally, we convinced her to take us to Mass where the priest blessed us with holy water. Frania also took us with her when she visited friends. When the other women criticized their employers, Frania never did so.

In our home, Frania was in charge of cooking as my mother was not especially interested in the activity. Each morning my mother discussed with Frania what they were going to prepare for dinner. My mother suggested something and when Frania disagreed, Frania would say: "The children and I don't like it." My mother usually let Frania make the choice.

We had a big cookbook that my mother rarely used. Once, when my parents were out of town, we talked Frania into baking chocolate cookies from the cookbook. As we read the ingredients of the recipe to her, Frania prepared the cookies. Evidently, we forgot to read some ingredients, so after the cookies were baked they did not look at all like the cookies in the cookbook. But, we had a good time and Frania didn't mind.

Frania often made noodles on a long table in the kitchen. She was a noodle artist: she worked quickly and it was fascinating for us children to watch. While she worked, I wrote letters for her to her boyfriend. As she made the noodles, she dictated what I should write to him. The letter always started with greetings and religious verses. At the end of one letter, I wrote, on my own initiative, "Please send me a present." Frania did not know I had done this. A week later, her boyfriend sent her a package of handkerchiefs, which we children quickly appropriated.

In our home, all the food was made from scratch including preserves, syrups, sauerkraut, pickled cucumbers, mushrooms, and smoked meat. Our household was like a small factory. Often, in the winter, poor people would knock at the door and ask my mother for syrup for their colds. My mother was a very generous woman and she always gave them raspberry syrup. She always said, "If someone puts out a hand, give him what he needs; don't ask, it's bad enough they have to do it at all."

When we made raspberry preserves, we children were seated around a long table, in the middle of which were piles of fresh raspberries. Every child had a big plate on which the raspberries were arranged with the opening up and it was our job to check the raspberries for spoilage and little green worms.

At this time, there were no appliances such as washers and dryers. Instead, Mrs. Mangold, who was a skilled laundry specialist, came in every six weeks to do the laundry. In my mother's dowry she had received twenty-four pieces of everything, so we had ample linens between laundry days. Frania cooked while Mrs. Mangold worked and they gossiped together about the doings and people in the city. After the clothes were washed, Mrs. Mangold hung them in the attic.

In the winter the clothes often froze on the clothesline. My father wore long underwear, which froze stiff into a walking position. We children played with the frozen clothing, making the long underwear walk around. One week after hanging up the laundry, Mrs. Mangold returned to take it down and iron it. The ironing took yet another week.

In the winter, which was usually very harsh, when we children had hopped into bed, Frania warmed our blankets in front of the tile oven. As she held the blankets near the oven, we children yelled, "Longer, longer!" When she determined the blankets were warm enough Frania quickly put them over us. Also during the winter Frania took us skating on a frozen lake in the park where, while we skated to the music, she met with her friends. When we became tired and chilled Frania was waiting for us with hot chocolate.

As a child, I had very long thick braids that reached to my waist. To my mind, no one but Frania could comb my hair the way I liked it. My mother tried hard, but Frania, after combing out my hair, always attached white bows that she had sprayed with a solution of water and sugar and ironed so that they would be stiff and beautiful. As a child I was often sick with sore throats. I always demanded to be paid before I would open my mouth for an examination.

Once when my parents were eating in a restaurant in Truskawiec, a resort city, my father asked the manager, "Who is your cook?" The manager replied that it was a Mrs. Jablonska. My father asked to meet her to thank her for the delicious dinner. When she came out, my father asked if she would like to cook for us. Mrs. Jablonskla agreed and she joined our household, too.

However, one day Frania took us for a walk and on our return she found Mrs. Jablonska sitting on top of the wardrobe with her feet hanging down! On the top of the wardrobe was a glass container with cherries in alcohol. Evidently, Mrs. Jablonska had climbed up onto the wardrobe, drunk too much, and couldn't get down. Frania helped to get her down and put her to bed to sober up. Until this time, when my father offered her a drink at dinner, Mrs. Jablonska had always refused saying "I don't drink." The next day my parents fired her.

Truskawiec was a city of flowers. On one visit, my father instructed Frania to get some ice cream for us and gave her some money to pay for it. However, we talked Frania into buying a whole meal for us at an expensive restaurant. When we were done eating,

The Bienstock family on vacation in Truskawiec, Poland

Frania found that she didn't have enough money to pay for the entire meal, so she paid for it with her own money and never told my parents.

Before we started formal schooling, we were schooled at home by Aunt Mala, my mother's aunt, a retired schoolteacher. (Both she and her sister were murdered by the Germans). She taught us how to read and write. I had tremendous difficulties writing the letters 'M' and 'N.' With her help, when I started first grade I was already able to read and write. Miss Roza, a friend of my mother's, also tutored us. She was divorced with two children and she needed money to support herself. She used to read *Les Miserablés* and the poems of Slowacki, a Polish poet, to us.

Even after we started formal schooling, we were still tutored by Miss Hania, a friend of my mother's. Miss Hania was very poor but when she received money from relatives in America for her dowry (which was necessary to get married) she gave it instead to her brother and his family who were even poorer. As a result, she never married and became a tutor to earn a living. She came to our home after school to supervise our homework. Frania always gave her tea and pastries. Sometimes I misinformed Miss Hania that I had no homework because I didn't like doing it. But Miss Hania discovered the truth from my friends, who were her next stop. By the time she was able to return to my house, I was already in bed fast asleep. So she completed my homework for me in my notebook. My parents never found out about it. This happened frequently.

My brother, Ludwik, loved to play soccer with his friends. I begged him to let me play with him, so they put me on the team as a goalie. My brother and his friends were all much larger than I and when the other team kicked in a goal which I could defend, my brother and his friends beat me up. I ran home crying where my mother and Frania scolded me: "Why do you play with them? They always beat you." The next day I did it again.

Chapter 4
Being Jewish in Drohobycz

Our home was observant. We children gladly followed religious rules. Together we approached every holiday with joyous anticipation. We were especially excited because we always got new clothing during the holidays.

Frania joined in with us on every religious occasion. Before the Sabbath, she helped my mother to prepare the Friday evening meal and set a beautiful table with a silver candelabra in the center.

My mother kept a kosher home and I have never seen a home prepared as beautifully and lovingly as my mother's was prepared for Passover. After cleaning the house thoroughly, every surface of our kitchen was covered by a special mat that we kept just for this purpose. From the attic, we brought down the special Passover dishes, utensils and silverware. Mother took us with her when she went to pick up the hand-made *matzah* and a kosher butcher delivered meat during the duration of Passover.

Mother told us stories about Passover, especially while we were in hiding. One was about "*Eliyahu Hanavi*" (Elijah) and involved a family's *seder* (supper) on the first night of Passover. As the family sat at the festive seder table, the father, as was the custom, filled a glass full to the brim with wine for Elijah. Custom dictates that the door is to be held open so that Elijah may come in and have a sip of it. Suddenly, a large house fly flew in, sat on the rim of the wineglass, and started to drink. The fly drank the entire cup to the very bottom. This visit by Elijah meant that the family was to be blessed with very good fortune and wealth.

Rosh Ha-Shanah and *Yom Kippur* were also big occasions in my home. My parents spent the entire day in the synagogue. After sundown we went with Frania to meet our parents near the synagogue with some drinks and cookies for them after fasting.

On *Hannukah* my father lit the candles and we sang holiday songs at *Purim*. We enjoyed watching the people dressed up in costumes and masks. Frania

PASSOVER AND THE HOLOCAUST

A few weeks before Passover, about 70 Jews in ... Bergen Belsen organized into a group ... to request flour for baking *matzot* in honor of the approaching Passover holiday. They addressed their written request to the camp commandant ... each of the 70 persons signed the petition.

Knowing from their past experience that the Germans set apart the Jewish holidays as days of terror, torture, and death, the 70 petition signers feared that they would probably be the Passover sacrifice, the Paschal lambs of Bergen Belsen.

Passover was only a few days away and the reply from Berlin had not yet arrived. At the height of their despair, when all hope appeared lost and a bitter fate seemed inevitable, two tall SS men with two huge dogs briskly entered ... They summoned the Rabbi of Bluzhow to the camp commandant ... Camp cap in hand, the rabbi stood before the commandant ... "As always, Berlin is generous with the Jews. You may bake your religious bread."

The building of the oven began with feverish haste, the Hasidim fearing that the camp commandant would change his mind at any minute ...the people were thrilled with the shapeless black *matzot*, especially for the children's sake that they might see and learn that a holiday is observed even in the Valley of Death.

Passover arrived. A *seder* was arranged in one of the barracks ... there was no shortage of bitter herbs; bitterness was in abundance. The suffering of the Jews was reflected in their eyes... The rabbi began to recite the *Haggadah* from memory.

He uncovered the *matzot*, lifted the ceremonial plate, and began to tell the story of the Exodus. "This is the bread of affliction that our fathers ate in the land of Egypt. All who are hungered—let them come and eat, all who are needy—let them come and celebrate Passover. Now we are here; next year may we be in the land of Israel! Now we are slaves; next year may we be free men!"

It was dark in the barracks. The moon's silvery, pale glow was reflected on the pale faces. It was as if the tears that silently streamed down their cheeks were flowing toward the lengedary angel with the huge jar of tears, which when filled to its brim would signal the end of human suffering.

As is customary, the rabbi began to explain the meaning of Passover in response to the Four Questions. But on that *seder* night in Bergen Belsen, the ancient questions of the *Haggadah* assumed a unique meaning. "Night," said the rabbi, "means exile, darkness, suffering. Morning means light, hope, redemption. Why is this night different from all other nights? Why is this suffering ... different from all the previous sufferings of the Jewish people?" No one attempted to respond to the rabbi's questions.

"For on all other nights we eat either bread or *matzah*, but tonight only *matzah*. Bread is leavened; it has height. *Matzah* is unleavened and is totally flat. During all our prevoius sufferings, during all our previous nights in exile, we Jews had bread and *matzah*. We had moments of bread, of creativity, and light, and moments of *matzah*, of suffering and despair. But tonight ... we experience our greatest suffering. We have reached the depths of the abyss, the nadir of humiliation. Tonight we have only *matzah*, we have no moments of relief, not a moment of respite for our humiliated spirits."

"We who are witness to the darknest night in history, the lowest moment of civilization, will also witness the great light of redemption...It was to us, my dear children, that our prophets have spoken, to us who dwell in the shadow of death, to us who will live to witness the great light of redemption."

The *seder* concluded. Somewhere above, the silvery glow of the moon was dimmed by dark clouds. The Rabbi of Bluzhow kissed each child on the forehead and reassured them that the darknest night of mankind would be followed by the brightest of all days.

As the children returned to their barracks, slaves of a modern Pharoah midst a desert of mankind, they were sure that the sounds of the Messiah's footsteps were echoing in the sounds of their own steps on the blood-soaked earth of Bergen Belsen.
(From: *Hasidic Tales of the Holocaust* by Yaffa Eliach)

baked delicious 'Haman's Ears' (*Hamantaschen*) for *Purim* that we always devoured greedily. The children made as much noise as possible when Haman's name was spoken with noisemakers called '*greger*' (Yiddish for 'noisemaker').

On *Simchas Torah*, we each got beautifully decorated flags with a red apple and a candle on top. Of course not all the Jewish children enjoyed holidays the way we did. Their parents couldn't afford it. Rabbi Rokach, who led our *stiebel*, couldn't make ends meet and sent his helper every Friday morning to my father for a donation. My father was always very generous.

This is our family home in Drohobycz today. It has been extensively remodeled, both inside and outside. When my family lived here there was no exit on this side of the house. The windows are new and have replaced the one we through which my father threw the clandestine furs into the arms of a Gestapo man. This picture was taken by Irene during her visit to Drohobycz in 2000.

54

Chapter 5
Life Under Russian Occupation:
1939-1941

On the first day of the war, my father was drafted into the Polish army as an officer. At the time, we had an automobile but my mother, like most women of her generation, didn't know how to drive. My father told her that if something happened, she should put everything in the car and find someone to drive it to Romania. When the war started, the Chief of Police of Drohobycz requested our car claiming that the Polish Army needed the vehicle. Instead, he took the car himself and fled to Romania with his own family. My father went to Przemysl where he joined his unit in which he commanded 120 soldiers.

During the first days of the war in September 1939 Drohobycz was heavily bombed by the Germans. Many of the neighbors on our street—assuming that it was safe because our house was new and built on a heavy foundation—came to us seeking shelter. Among them was Miss Genia, an older woman. The first day Miss Genia spent with us, Frania's sister, Marysia, told her that if she would soak herself in water for a few hours the gas from the bombs would not touch her. What she really wanted her to do was to take a bath because she did not smell good. The next time Miss Genia took shelter with us, we noticed that her fingers were wrinkled from the water.

In the beginning of 1939, my mother's brother, Mano, who lived in Leipzig, Germany with his family was expelled to Poland with his wife and two daughters, who were the same age as my sister and myself. They stayed with my family for eight months and left just before the outbreak of the war. My Uncle Mano, who was quite wealthy, enrolled his daughters in school in England and arranged for his wife to accompany them as a governess. From England they all emigrated to the United States where they survived the war.

In 1939, shortly after the beginning of the war, a tragedy struck our family. My brother, Ludwik, became sick with pneumonia. Irene was present when, she told me later, he was laughing and talking and suddenly he said, "I don't feel so good." And then he was gone. He was thirteen years old. When Marysia,

Frania's sister, saw what happened, she called my mother. My mother, in shock, started screaming so loudly that I think the whole street came running to our home.

My father and I arrived home after my brother had already

Irene in the room where Lukwik died in 1939

died. My parents and Frania walked in the funeral procession for my brother. Ludwik was really my mother's and Frania's favorite child and my mother never recovered from his death. Sometimes when Ludwik came home from school he would take out a piece of dirty paper out of his pocket in which some sticky candies were wrapped and proudly give it to Frania. This made her very happy.

Compounding this tragedy, in the first days of the war, when Lvov was bombed by German airplanes, my mother's youngest sister, Hela, was killed in the attack. She had been married just a few months and after searching relentlessly for her, her husband finally found her in the morgue several days later. Then six weeks after my brother passed away, my father's father died of a broken heart as a result of the death of his only grandson. Thus, our family sat in continuous *shivah* (mourning) for three weeks after the death of my aunt, my brother, and my grandfather.

Before Germany invaded Poland in September 1939, Germany and Russia had made an secret agreement to split Poland between them. In one of the points of the treaty, Stalin agreed that Russia would not enter any war against Germany. Germany was to get the western half of Poland and the eastern half was to go to Russia. The part of Poland we lived in was in the Russian portion.

Immediately after Russian soldiers marched into Drohobycz, they came to our house and announced that we could not live alone in such a big house. They promptly assigned two NKVD (the Russian secret police) men and their families to live with us.

The situation under the Russians was difficult. My father's business was taken away from him and he had no income. He was given a special passport by the Russians which had a paragraph in it that described him as an "undesirable element." This designation kept him from getting a good job. We, as an "undesirable element," had to leave our home in Drohobycz and everything in it was confiscated by the Russians. We went to Truskawiec, a nearby resort town, where my parents rented a house in which we lived for several months. From there we went to Boryslaw, where my mother's younger sister and her family lived. During the entire time of the Russian occupation, we stayed in constant touch with Frania.

Irene on the street in modern day Drohobycz where our father had his shop.

Under Russian occupation, life was fairly quiet. In Boryslav I went to a Russian school for one year. I was very disappointed that I was not accepted to the Pioneers, a youth club. As a capitalist, my father was not considered to be a good element, so I, as his daughter, was refused.

THE TASTE OF SWEETS

This time of year in December it is a pleasure to go shopping. People of all denominations celebrate and the malls are beautifully decorated. As I do my holiday shopping my first steps turn toward the Lady Godiva. What a display of sweets!

Even today as an elderly lady I cannot resist sweets. I have always liked candies and chocolate in any form. As a child I could not pass by a candy store without making even the smallest purchase. In my lifetime I have lived in several countries—Poland, Germany, Israel, the United States—and traveled to many more. I have enjoyed different kinds of sweets in each. Yet there is one particular candy that I tasted more than fifty years ago. I remember the color, shape, and flavor, although I held it in my mouth for only a brief moment. Let me tell you the story.

It was in Drohobycz, Poland where I was born and lived with my parents and older sister during World War II. Due to the fact that we were Jewish, we were persecuted by the Nazis. We were poor and all things of value were taken away from us. My father, once a wealthy and prominent businessman, performed forced labor while my mother sold the remainder of our clothes and household items and invented new dishes consisting mostly of potatoes and grain. We still lived in our home but we now shared that home with several other families. Each family occupied one room. Today, after so many years, I lack words to describe the living conditions. They seem improbable even to me. We, the children, were not allowed to attend school and lived in constant fear of our lives. We witnessed the death of many family and friends.

One day I went to visit my best friend Bianka, who lived nearby with her parents. I remember her so well, although she was killed more than fifty years ago. She was tall and slim with black pigtails. On that particular day Bianka's mother surprised me by offering me a candy. I remember the candy very well. It was yellow and square and tasted so good. What a delight! After one second I turned around, took the candy from my mouth and made sure

that no one witnessed my conduct. I excused myself, went to the bathroom, rinsed the almost intact candy, and wrapped it in some paper. I soon
left my friend's house. At home I gave the candy
to my sister and told her that I was given several
of them.

These many years later, I believe this was the
biggest sacrifice I ever made. After all, I was
ten years old, and I loved candies.

Irene Frisch, copyright 1992

A page from Pola's diary that she started during her family's final departure from Drohobycz after liberation. It was written on the back of a Russian invoice as no other paper was available.

Chapter 6
The Germans Return to Drohobycz

We stayed in Boryslaw until 1941 when Germany broke the treaty with Russia and invaded her former ally. Thus, the Germans returned to our part of Poland and drove the Russians out. Boryslaw, where we stayed with my aunt, was also surrounded by oil wells and refineries. Before the Russians were driven out, they tried to destroy the wells and refineries so the Germans would not get the oil. They threw grenades into the wells and refineries and the fires quickly spread to the city, which began to burn fiercely. Many people, driven out of their houses by the flames, stood in the middle of the street as their city burned around them. The wells and refineries burned for several months.

The first thing the Germans did upon taking over Drohobycz for the second time was to give the local people a free hand again for twenty-four hours to do anything they wanted with the Jews. The local people, both Poles and Ukrainians, again killed many Jews and robbed their homes.

Eventually we returned from Boryslav to our home in Drohobycz. Before we had left Drohobycz, my father had hidden some furs and little by little we sold them. However, it was a strict German law that all the Jews had to turn over all their furs and jewelry to them. If the Germans caught anyone with forbidden goods, it was a death sentence. One night, my father brought twenty-four skins home. He had made arrangements for someone to pick them up early the next morning. Shortly after his arrival with the contraband furs, our front door reverberated with a strong knocking. It was the Gestapo! My father grabbed the furs and threw them out the window into the sideyard of the house next door where non-Jews lived. What we didn't know was that our entire house was surrounded and the furs unfortunately fell directly on one of the Gestapo men's head. A few minutes later, he entered the house with the furs. That evening we were lucky. My father paid the Gestapo men off and they left with the furs. We could easily have been shot.

Shortly after taking over in June 1941, the Germans began murdering Jews. First, they rounded up elderly people who could not work and were considered useless mouths. My mother's aunt, who was staying with us, was directed to report to the Germans. My mother begged her to stay with us, but she insisted that she had to go. She, and other elderly Jews, were shot and buried in mass graves in the forest of Bronica, outside the city. Before they were shot, they were forced to undress so their clothes could be sent to German families. It is a mystery to me that the German civilians claim "We did not know what was going on." What did they think of the origin of the clothing, footwear, and jewelry that was being handed out to them?

Next the Germans rounded up and began to murder the Jewish children. My father's only brother, Max, had three daughters. His two older daughters were deported to the Janowska concentration camp near Lvov, where they were both murdered. Uncle Max, his wife, and his youngest daughter, Roza, lived with us in our home. Roza and her mother were both murdered by the Germans. Roza was ten years old. She loved to knit and had made a beautiful pair of red- and yellow-striped mittens. When the trucks returned from the forest, without the people but piled high with discarded clothing, I saw those red- and yellow-striped mittens perched on top of one of those piles. The rough motion of the truck caused them to fall to the ground.

Work was the key to survival so my father arranged a work pass for me. The minimum age for a work permit was sixteen years of age. Although I was only twelve, I looked older because I was tall and skinny. I got a job in a riding school where the Gestapo men taught their wives and children how to ride horses. I carried bricks to build the riding school. Across the street from the riding school lived a Gestapo man named Karl Günter. When his girlfriend came to visit, together with another Gestapo man named Landau, he taught her how to shoot from the balcony of his apartment. For target practice she killed three or four Jews who worked at the riding school.

My father worked for a German company and was lodged on site. My mother, myself and my sister were visiting him in his room when the Gestapo suddenly swarmed in to arrest us. Apparently, someone had denounced us. My mother became very frightened and ran. A Gestapo man shot her in the breast and she fell. As

Irene in the doorway of the house where our
mother, Sara Bienstock, was shot by the Gestapo
in 1942.

she lay bleeding on the ground, the Gestapo took the rest of us away. My mother got up and crept home.

She feared that we would never return—that the Gestapo would kill us. Meantime, the rest of us were taken to the Gestapo headquarters where my father explained in good German that he and Irene were employed at a German company and that I worked at the riding school. It was apparently convincing enough and they let us go. It was very unusual to leave the Gestapo headquarters alive.

When we arrived home, my mother was sitting in the doorway of our home, crying and talking to herself, "They are all killed, they are all dead, they are all killed." My father took her to a Jewish physician who took care of her.

Another time, during an *Aktion* while I was working at the riding school, someone came and said that the Bienstock family had been rounded up and were being taken to the forest to be shot. Although there was another family called Bienstock in the city, I thought it was my family. In a frenzy, I ran out into the street after the departing trucks which were carrying the Jews to the forest to be murdered. I wanted

70

to die with my family. Mr. Backenrot, a Jewish
engineer at the riding school, caught me by the
collar, like a dog, and pulled me back. In the
meantime, someone had told my parents of the incident. When I discovered my error and returned home
I found my parents weeping. They thought I had been
caught and murdered.

I also worked as a maid for a German family named
Klopfenburg from Hamburg. The wife was deliberately
cruel to me, ordering me time and again to return
and redo something I had already done as her own
children of my age played in the yard.

Once, two Ukrainian girls from the Sribny family
paid us a visit. One had been a schoolmate of mine
and the other was several years older. Their father
was a judge. They boldly rang the front doorbell of
our home and when my mother opened the door, they
asked that my mother give them the beautiful plants
she kept in the house because the Germans were going
to "kill you anyway." The older sister was very
friendly with the Gestapo and often rode horses with
them. After the war, she settled near New York,
married a physician, and became part of Ukrainian
high society.

One day a little boy carrying an empty cup came to the balcony of our home and cried in Yiddish, "Mrs. Bienstock, please, I am so hungry." My mother filled his cup with our regular soup made of flour and water.

During one *Aktion*, my desperate father went to the mayor of the city, Mr. Kostrzemski, with whom he was friends and begged him to hide us. The mayor agreed for altruistic reasons and without being paid and told my father to bring us to the City Hall where we hid for one week in the clock tower. Every hour the clock rang loudly. As a result, my mother's hearing became permanently impaired.

From the windows of the clock tower we could see everything that was going on in the city: who killed whom, who robbed whom. We were witnesses to everything that happened. German police and their helpers, the Ukrainians, rounded up Jewish adults and children. For each Jew they flushed out of hiding they received 500 *zlotys*, the price of a loaf of bread.

The mayor confided in his servant about our presence in the City Hall and asked him to feed us. Everyday

Irene in front of City Hall where we were hidden
in the clock tower by the mayor of Drohobycz.

this well-meaning man brought us Napoleons (cream-filled pastries). We had nothing else for seven days—just Napoleons and water. Today I cannot stand the sight of Napoleons.

Eventually, the Germans created a formal ghetto in the city to contain the remaining Jews who had not been shot in the woods. We were forced to leave our house and move into the ghetto, which was in Lany, the poor part of the city near the Jewish cemetery. There was insufficient food and we had to share the house with a number of other people. Each family got one room. My father's brother lived with us and every night he cried terribly. His entire family had already been murdered. My father began to break up our furniture to be used as firewood. The furniture that had escaped German confiscation or being burnt as firewood was used by my mother to barter for food with nearby Polish farmers.

At this time, my father was approached by a wealthy Polish woman who wanted to buy our house. She offered my father 500 dollars even though our house was worth much more. Since we had to move to the ghetto, my father reluctantly sold her the house. After the war, this Polish woman could not keep the house because the Russians took it over. She went to Krakow, from which she sent her son to my father to demand that he return her money with interest. The son stayed with us for several days, during which my father treated him with great courtesy. When he left my father sent the money with him to his mother. She didn't deserve the return of the money. She took advantage of our vulnerable situation, hoping for gains.

GRAND DAME: A TALE OF WARTIME GREED

"I met a real 'grand dame' today," said my father upon returning home on a summer afternoon in 1942. "A 'grand dame,' from real gentility," he said to my mother.

I looked up, my eyes diverted for the moment from the book that I was reading-since I could not go to school I devoured any book that I could get my hands on. I listened intently to my parents' conversation.

I wanted to know what a grand dame was, since my recent experience with people was quite different. For the last two years my father had not earned any money, although he worked every day. We supported ourselves by selling off our possessions, which became fewer and fewer. The Nazi soldiers would enter Jewish homes, taking away people to be killed, and grabbing their possessions. As a result there was less and less to be sold. Fortunately my mother still had some jewelry left, and we suffered less than others.

I found out that the grand dame, a Mrs. O., was interested in buying fine jewelry. She was a wealthy non-

Jewish woman with two teenage children. Due to some old family connections she held an important position in the salt-mine industry, and was able to divert a substantial amount of salt for sale on the black market. In those days, salt was a very valuable commodity, especially for the local farmers, so one could earn a healthy profit from such activities.

Within the next few months, my father paid many visits to Mrs. O. He sold her the rest of my mother's jewelry, including a ring that I had always admired, with my mother's initials inscribed in sapphires and diamonds.

Father also helped our neighbors and friends to dispose of their jewelry. Mrs. O. was a willing buyer with excellent taste. The prices she offered were usually very low, as people were desperate and needed money to buy food and to bribe their persecutors. Father paid his visits in the evenings, in disguise, and entered through the back door of her house. After every trip, Father remarked at how grand she was indeed, in both her manners and her elegant dwelling.

Mrs. O. always offered him a glass of tea in fine china. She asked him to sit down in her living room and served him cake. To my father, who now lived in the most shabby conditions, this was quite a treat.

Although she was a grand dame, Mrs. O. never in-quired about our family. When I listened to Father's stories, I always imagined that one day Mrs O. would send a candy or a cookie for my sister and me. After all, I was only 11 years old and we were surviving on bread, potatoes, and water.

One day, while speaking with my father, Mrs. O. inquired about our pre-war home. In 1938, my par-ents had built a custom-designed one-family house on a lot that my mother had inherited. It was a luxurious modern villa, and the architect who had designed and contracted it for us was still alive in the ghetto.

A few evenings later, my father, the architect-who before the war had been a very reputable man in our town-and a lawyer, went together to Mrs. O.'s home. They presented her with some facts and figures on the villa, and a deal was made. My father had spent about $40,000 on the construction.The lawyer wrote a contract according to which my father sold the house to Mrs. O. for $500. After the war, if we were not to survive, the house would be hers for the $500. However, if we did survive, we could buy it back from her within six months for $5,000 in American currency.

This deal was, of course, no deal, since it was obvious that even if we survived the war, there was no chance that we could raise the $5,000 within six months. And if we could not come up with this amount, our villa would remain hers for her initial payment of $500.

This small amount did help us to survive for a short time. Soon afterward, father was sent to a concentration camp, and my mother, sister, and I went into hiding.

After the liberation in the summer of 1944, we three women emerged, starved, rising from the ashes, nearly dead physically and spiritually. There was no word from our father. We had no way of knowing whether he was even alive. We were so frightened that we did not dare to go to our old house, which was now inhabited by the strangers who had rented it from Mrs. O.

After six months, Mrs. O. paid a visit to our shabby one-room apartment. My mother worked odd jobs in order to support us. We were very poor. I remember vividly Mrs. O.'s arrival. It was the first time that I had seen her. She made a striking entrance, dressed elegantly, just as a grand dame would. Without even sitting down, she asked my mother if she was ready to pay the $5,000 to buy back the house. Mrs. O. did not inquire how we have survived, or even whether my father was alive. She walked out the happy owner of a house for $500.

In 1945, due to the terms of the Yalta Conference, we were all forced to leave our part of Poland and were relocated to another area. Mrs. O. left the town in a grand style, accompanied by servants and fancy luggage. Among her valuable papers was a worthless contract for a house for $500.

We were soon reunited with our father, who had miraculously survived. Being a skilled business-man, he was able to start all over, and in short time we were living a quite comfortable lifestyle and managing to save some money.

So one day a young man arrived at our house. He was the son of Mrs. O., a student at the university in the big city where Mrs. O.'s family had resettled. He brought a letter from his mother, who demanded $500 from us. She insisted that since political exigencies had forced her to abandon the villa she had bought from us, she was now entitled to the return of her initial $500. She made no mention of any relevant conditions or stipulations.

My father, an honorable and good-natured man, de-cided to repay her. He asked the son of Mrs. O. to stay with us for a few days while my father raised the necessary amount and converted it into Ameri-can dollars. Back then, this was a small fortune. Father also noted that the young Mr. O. could use a new suit, so he bought one for him. Father also bought a beautiful gift for Mrs. O.

Many years passed. We moved to different parts of the world. My parents died long ago. I started a new life in the United States and, upon my retirement in 1989, I began to travel. Last summer, while I was on vacation with my husband in Czechoslovakia, I became obsessed with the idea of visiting the country of my birth. We rented a car and visited Cracow, one of the biggest Polish cities.

While unpacking in the hotel, I was overcome with emotion. Suddenly I remembered that this was the city were Mrs. O. had resettled and where her son had attended the university. Many memories rushed back and I realized for the first time that the grand dame was not a lady, but a phony opportunist who thrived on other people's misery.

I was tempted to see Mrs. O. Perhaps I wanted to reconnect with that part of my childhood. I also thought to try to buy back my mother's ring. I opened the telephone book and found the number of the young Mr. O.

His wife answered the phone, and after I introduced myself, she told me that her husband had died two years earlier. Mrs. O. had passed away a few years before that. We met with the daughter-in-law of Mrs. O. and discovered that Mrs. O. had treated her own son shabbily too. She had been disappointed when he did not meet her grandiose expectations and instead married beneath him, the girl he loved, who was from much humbler circumstances. After he had finished at the university, he operated a small business, publishing fine art books, and was never a great financial success.

Seeing that her son had failed to establish a brilliant career, Mrs. O. disinherited him and even cheated him out of an inheritance that was due to him from his father's estate. She favored instead her daughter, who had met her expectations by marrying a physician. On his deathbed, the son had written, "I was not the only one that my mother took advantage of."

I was probably not meant to ever meet a really grand dame. I now hope that I will never meet one I am better off with people of modest means and ideas.
Irene Frisch

OUR STRADIVARIUS

Lately, with all the terrible things going on in the world, I find that reading the newspapers—once a favorite daily routine—is not a pleasant activity anymore. However, on April 13, 2002, an interesting headline in the New York Times caught my eye: "AN UPPER EAST SIDE MYSTERY. THE VANISHED STRADIVARIUS."

Apparently, a rare Stradivarius violin, worth $1.6 million, was stolen from the workshop of a violin-maker near Lincoln Center. An old memory, buried for over 50 years, stirs within me: my family's 'Stradivarius.'

It was Poland, 1945, shortly after the end of World War II. Now that so much has been said and written about the Holocaust and its aftermath, I will spare you the details of our ordeal. Briefly, our Jewish family miraculously survived. Our father returned from the concentration camps, my mother, sister and I came out of hiding, and we resumed a normal life. Normal? Our parents desperately tried to make it normal and my sister and I cooperated.

We were forced to leave our hometown, as that part of Poland was now in Russia. We traveled by cattle cars to a newly-assigned part of Europe, which was previously Germany and was now Poland. After several weeks of traveling, we were assigned to a town called Legnica.

Father, once a successful fur trader who had traveled to England, Germany, Sweden and Russia before the War to attend fur auctions, now opened a small store below our apartment. He traded in everything possible, buying and selling, in order to feed our family. The town was occupied by the Russian army. Soldiers were robbing, stealing, and acquiring goods in any possible way. Also, some people were selling off their possessions in order to buy food. Others were buying.

One day a Russian soldier appeared in father's store, probably in need of some money to buy vodka. He offered my father an old violin. Father, who played the violin, showed some interest. He in-spected the instrument and discovered, inside, some letters. Taking a closer look, father saw the name "Stradivarius." Father knew the significance of the name and bought the violin immediately. He closed the store down in the middle of the day and came up to the apartment. He pulled down the shades of our apartment, gathered the family around the table and made an announcement: "Today we became very, very rich. We have a violin worth hundreds of thousands of dollars which will enable us to have a secure future. We will try to go abroad. We will be able to buy a house, start a business, and pay tuition in the best schools." After that, we were not allowed to talk about the violin. We were very happy with our good fortune; we lived in a state of euphoria.

A few days later, Father wanted more reassurance. There was no way to verify the authenticity of the violin. My parents devised a plan. There was a Jewish piano teacher who also had survived the war. He lived with the family of a violin teacher. My parents invited both men for Sunday dinner.

When the meal was over Father pulled down the shades, locked the doors, and swore them both to secrecy. He showed them the violin.

The verdict: It was a cheap violin, made for beginning students with the extravagant name "Stradivarius" printed on it for show. What a letdown.

Our family resumed its modest existence. Still we managed to go abroad, to afford tuition to good schools, and to achieve our dreams even without the violin. But our big dream—of the 'Stradivarius' and its great fortunes—proved to be a dream only. Or was it?

Today I wonder: maybe it was the real thing? We know that many objects of art were looted during World War II. Maybe father's violin—whose eventual destination I cannot recall today—was one such object? After all, how much could the teacher from a small town in Poland know about a Stradivarius violin?

Irene Frisch, April 14, 2002

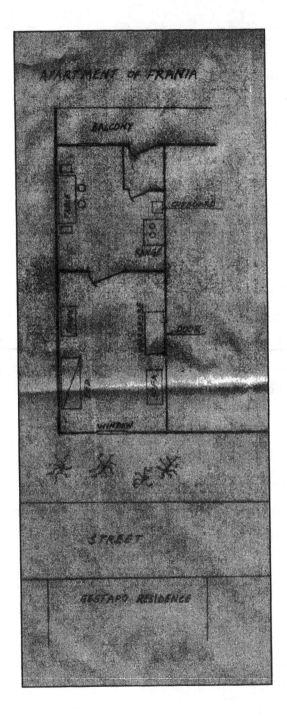

The floor plan
of Frania's
apartment where
we were hidden
during the war.

Chapter 7
Frania Hides Us in Her Home

After we moved into the ghetto, Frania came and asked my mother to give her the children only. This was a very dangerous thing to do because if the Germans had caught her in the ghetto, they would have shot her and us on the spot. My mother consented and Frania took Irene with her to her small apartment. Irene stayed with Frania for a few months alone. Eventually, my mother joined her.

It is hard to imagine today that a child could stay alone in an apartment without any means of amusing himself or herself without books, toys, radio, and so on. Frania left at six o'clock every morning to go to work as a cook for a Gestapo man and returned twelve hours later. Frania's return home each day was the highlight of Irene's life.

The rumors increased that the ghetto would soon be liquidated. At this time, my father finally decided for me to go to Frania and join mother and Irene. Before we left for Frania's, father got some potatoes that he cooked for dinner. After the potatoes were cooked, I had to drain the hot water, which I did not know how to do. My father was very upset that a girl this age did not know how to do such a simple chore. Finally, we did it together. It is amazing to me today that such a trivial thing could upset my father at this time.

The safest time and route not to be detected was at midnight through the Jewish cemetery. I had never been in the cemetery before. Like all children we told each other scary tales about ghosts and cadavers coming out of their graves. I held strongly to my father's hand, shivering with fear. The journey seemed to be endless. Under cover of darkness, we arrived at Frania's apartment and again we had to be very careful not to be seen by her neighbors. At last, we arrived at her apartment and I was reunited with my mother and Irene.

Frania's apartment had a short entry hall, a kitchen, and one other room. In the main room there was door, behind which lived another gentile family. Each apartment had a separate entrance. My father could not stay with Frania because he was a heavy smoker and had a bad cough that would have given us away to the family next door.

My mother, Irene, and I had to be quiet as mice so they would not hear us during the day. While we were in hiding with Frania, my father returned to the camp in the city. Later he was transferred to a camp in Boryslav from which he escaped and hid in the forest.

One day in the forest he met a very poor man, a Seventh Day Adventist, who took my father into his meager shelter. My father sent him for help to the mayor of Drohobycz, Mr. Kostrzemski (the same man who had hidden our entire family in the City Hall). He loaded him up with food and told him: "Take good care of this man. He will one day repay your generosity." On another occasion, the same man appeared at Frania's apartment to ask for help. He needed money to buy food for our father. For us it was a feast to know that our father was still alive. A short time later, my father was captured by the Germans and was deported to a concentration camp.

While we were in hiding, my father's only brother, Max, was stopped on the street by the Gestapo. His wife and daughter, Roza, had already been murdered in the forest of Bronica and his two other daughters had been deported to Janowska concentration camp. Since he knew what was coming, he tried to run, and was shot on the spot. His body lay for several days in the streets. Frania saw his body on the street but she didn't tell us about it for a long time. We wouldn't have been able to bury him anyway. What a sad end for an innocent human being.

Frania loved to interpret dreams and each morning during breakfast she asked us about our dreams. If you dreamed about blood it meant good news was coming; if you dreamed about fire it meant something would be stolen. If something was lost and could not be found, the best solution was to turn over a glass and the lost item would come to you. Shortly after my arrival Frania had an unusual dream in which my mother's mother, with whom she was close, had told her: "Take good care of them. Nothing will happen to you."

Frania also believed strongly in the "evil eye." Ludwik was her favorite child and when he was not feeling well Frania believed it was because someone was jealous of his beauty and intelligence and had cast an "evil eye" upon him. In such cases she took a glass of water and performed a special ritual. Into the glass of water she put several small pieces of charcoal. If the charcoal fell to the bottom it was a sure sign that he had the "evil eye." She then wet her fingers in the water, touched Ludwik's forehead with her hand and then threw the charcoal into the four corners of the room.

We had no newspapers or other means of obtaining information about the current condition of the war. Frania would call through the door to the other family and ask, "Where are the armies now?" When they answered, we listened and that is how we learned about the progress of the war.

Frania's sister, Hania, who had married an Ukrainian man, came to us during the German occupation and said she had a place she could hide us if it became necessary. She said that she needed some of our household furnishings in order to set it up. A few weeks later, when the first *Aktion* occurred, she did not come to get us. I think that we were lucky that we didn't go with her because her husband would have killed us. This happened many times to Jews in hiding.

When Frania learned of this betrayal, she was very angry. When her sister came to visit her one day (we were hiding in the other room and her sister didn't know we were there), Frania told her what she thought about her having left us to die after taking our things. Frania told her that she never wanted to see her, her husband, or her children again. She was not her sister any more.

During this time, when Frania cooked for the Gestapo man she always wore an apron with a hidden pocket. During the day, she ferreted away candies, cookies, and sugar into the pocket and we waited like eager little dogs for her to come home each night with the treats. During Passover, while we were in hiding at Frania's, we celebrated Passover the best way we could: we had no bread so for seven days we ate only potatoes.

Once Frania was able to get an inexpensive loaf of bread that was a little moldy. My sister Irene didn't want to eat it. My mother, against the advice of today's psychiatrists, said to her "If you don't eat it you will die and what are we going to do with your body here?" Irene ate the bread.

The situation was very uncertain. When my sister and I asked my mother "What will happen to us?" My mother's reply was often the same: "It always cannot be bad. It has to improve."

Frania's mother and brother knew about what Frania was doing for us. While we were in hiding, Frania's mother always reminded her to leave water for us. She also made us bread occasionally, even though she was very poor. She put everything she had in it including potatoes, cabbage, and flour. Frania's brother brought it to us, but he was so frightened that he always left it near Frania's door and ran off.

While we were in hiding we had no books, toys, or newspapers—nothing with which to occupy ourselves. My mother told us stories about people in our city to wile away the time. To pass the time I wrote childish poems and pretended to be a cook by concocting some fanciful recipes. Some of my recipes were:

Pancakes: Boil pieces of old linoleum in tomato sauce; let them cool down; then spread sauerkraut on them; roll and fry.

Good minced scallop: Take the skin off a fat rat; grind the meat; add a pinch of ashes and marmalade; mix and fry in lice fat.

Lemonade: Juice from an old bull, mix with water; add some corn flour; then milk from two canaries; boil together and let cool down. More details at Ms. Kasia Pyskacz's

Cheap aspic: Tablespoon of raspberries, tablespoon of mushrooms, pinch of pepper, a tail and a head of a herring: mix together; put into a washing basin; pour buttermilk over it and fry in dog's fat. After scorching, decorate with [illegible.]

On 25 June 1943 I wrote this poem entitled "*Freedom.*" I signed the poem "Sylwester Ostozny" who was a comic character (much like Mickey Mouse) in Poland.

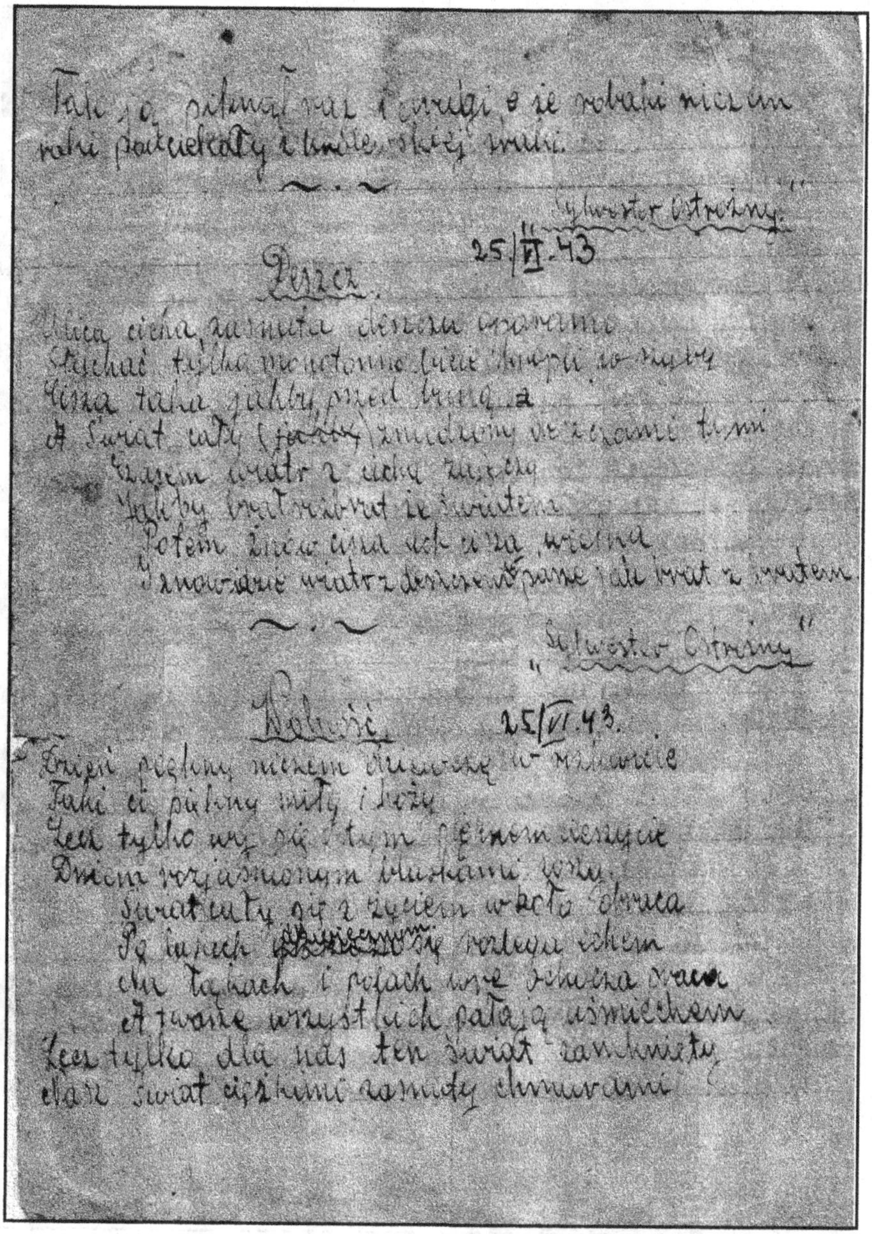

A page from Pola's writings while she was in hiding.

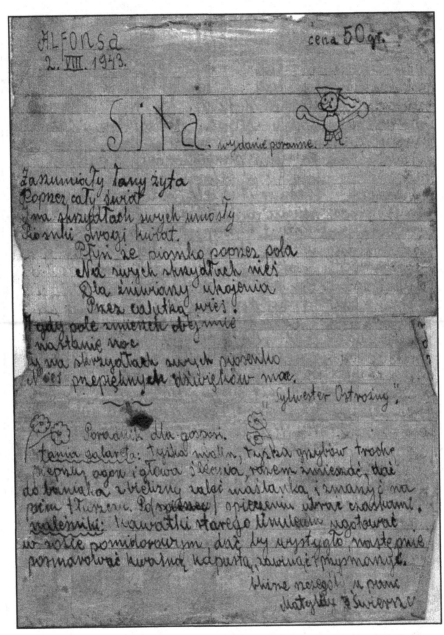

A page from Pola's writings while she was in hiding.

98

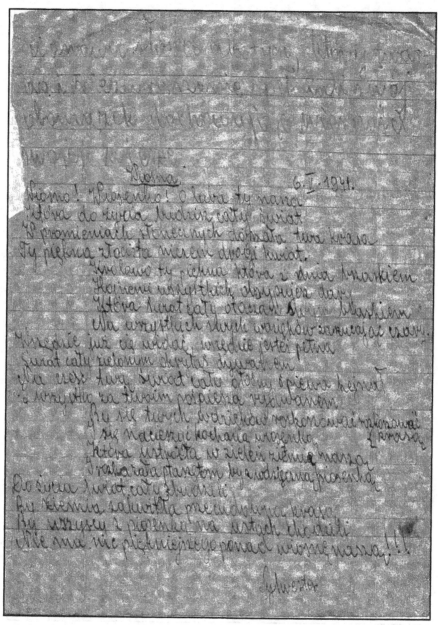

A page from Pola's writings while she was in hiding.

Potem głęboko w oczy mi spojrzysz
I więcej naszych nie będziesz deptał
Lecz niema już Ciebie, ciebie mój drogi
Odeszłeś tak licho i niespodziewanie
Nie wstępując nawet w mego domu progi
Niechże wróci do mnie Ciebie proszę Panie.
Niech wróci do mnie i już nie odleci
Do końca życia tego naszego
Życiu naszem niech gwiazdą przewodzi!
Boże! Niech wróci ja czekam na niego

"Sylwester strózy"

Niewola

W kajdanach ciężkiej niewoli
Siedzę i myślę o pięknym świecie
To mej strażnej nie ludzkiej doli
Siedzę i czekam!
Siedzę i czekam i myślę że przecie
Się wydostanę kiedyś z tego piekła
Że są jeszcze ludzie na tym Bożym świecie
Siedzę i myślę że wyjdę stąd przecie!
Siedzę! Ali się jeszcze we mnie nabija
Że będę oglądać jeszcze piękny ten świat
Że zmieni to wszystko ręką czarodzieja
I jeden drugiemu będzie niczem brat
Siedzę i myślę, a myśli me płyną
Płyną falą wielką niosem bystra rzeka

A page from Pola's writings while she was in hiding.

100

Freedom

Day beautiful, like a girl in full bloom
So beautiful, nice and lovely
But only you are enjoying this beauty
On a day brightened with the glow of dawn.
    The whole world spins around lively
      In the forest reverberates a sonorous echo
      On the meadows and fields brisk work is in
         full swing
      And everyone's face is aglow with smiles.
But for us only, that world is closed
Our world is covered with heavy clouds
We are the nation forevermore damned
Approaching calamity with great steps.
      Our world is a train of serious torments
      Our world is an abyss in the depths of which
      Live our souls full of sacrifices
      With this thought that maybe someday and
        for them
The sun will flare up like a star in the sky
That they will be able to walk around with a
    smile
Across this God's world
And this laughter will reverberate with echo
      That breeze of joy will scatter our sorrows

Which like a reptile creeps into our bones
That with free hearts and at liberty
We will be dreaming about the great future.

(More of Pola's poems can be found in the Appendix at the back of this book.)

Irene and I also fantasized that we would grow up in hiding and become unrecognizable and would be able to walk free.

One day Frania took a big chance and invited a neighbor to her apartment in a calculated move to allay suspicions. My mother hid in the wardrobe and Irene and I hid in a trunk. When the woman came into the main room, Frania casually asked her if she thought it needed painting. From our hiding places, we heard the woman reply that she thought it looked fine. We were all worried that we would sneeze or make a noise, but the visit went off fine and the woman left unaware that there were three other people in the apartment with Frania.

During this time Frania met a man who worked in the local mill. He was stealing flour from his employers and he brought it to Frania in a big sack. We divided it into small portions and Frania sold it on the black market. Looking back, this was not very smart because if the man had been followed to Frania's apartment we would have been caught and killed. Once when we divided up the flour, we made a mistake in calculating the price and told Frania that she owed him ten *zlotys*. In reality the amount should have been twelve *zlotys*. There followed a long discussion between him and Frania about the discrepancy in the price. From the other room, we overheard the discussion and belatedly realized that he was right although, of course, we could not tell Frania about it. Eventually, the man accepted the ten *zlotys* and left. We told Frania about our mistake and she paid him the other two *zlotys* the next day.

We were hungry a lot of the time. One night Frania could not sleep from hunger. She found a little flour in the house and made some noodles. Instead of eating them alone, she woke us children and shared them with us.

One day there was a loud knock at the door. "Who is it?" Frania asked. "Police," came the answer. It is impossible to imagine the deadly fear that embraced us. We ran to the window and prepared to jump out

Irene in front of the house where we were hidden by Frania
during the war.

while Frania delayed opening the door. Then the
voice, which belonged to Frania's neighbor, said
"Mrs. Sobkowa, I was just joking!"

My mother had a large family. She had five brothers: Mano, who lived in Germany; Max, who lived in
Amsterdam; Elias, who also lived in Germany;
Herschel, who lived in Drohobycz; and Maurice, who
died before my birth. Mano was wealthy and he was
able to survive by immigrating to the United States

with his family via England. My mother's older brother, Herschel, was married to Frieda, and they had four daughters. Their two oldest daughters survived the war but the two youngest, Roza and Sala, were murdered. One of the two older girls survived the war in Russia and the other survived the camp system. Herschel and Frieda were murdered by the Germans.

My mother also had three sisters: the youngest, Hela, was killed on the first day of the war when the Germans bombed Lvov. She was twenty-four years old and had just been married. Another sister, Pearl, and her husband and son were murdered by the Germans. Tosia, my mother's other sister, her husband and son, survived the war.

ANNE FRANK AND ME

To break the monotony of the long car ride, I listen to the radio. I select a station at random, with nothing special in mind and catch a narrator in mid-sentence. After a moment, I realize that he is speaking about Anne Frank. March marks the fiftieth anniversary of the young girl's death. The media is seizing upon this story, but many of us already feel we know all there is to know about the Holocaust, having read books and seen movies—most recently *Schindler's List*.

A voice on the radio reads excerpts from Anne Frank's diary, adding his own comments. The voice is sympathetic and sad, as befits the occasion. It is touching to listen to the young girl's feelings, hopes, thoughts, dreams, and about her life in hiding, especially since we know that she will eventually meet a horrible death at a tender age.

To me Anne Frank's story has special meaning. We are soul sisters. I think of a childhood friend—who like Anne—did not survive World War II, but perished at the age of 12. As I listen to the diary excerpts, I also reflect on my own years during the war. Like Anne, I went into hiding with my older sister and mother. We also had our squabbles, misunderstandings, and did not venture out of doors for roughly two-and-one-half years. Anne's thoughts and feelings are too familiar to me. I missed my freedom during the war, and could not understand why people hated each other believing that people are truly good.

I was fortunate to have a loving mother and sister. We entertained each other as best we could. My mother told us stories from her life, of different events and people in our hometown while my sister and I shared our fears, hopes and plans for the future. We also played our favorite game, asking each other "What will happen when the war ends and we are free?" We believed and hoped that the world would compensate us for the injustices we endured.

In the summer of 1944, our town was liberated by the Russian army. My family was accused of conspiring with the Nazis; how else, demanded the Russians, were we able to survive? We were shocked by our rescuers' accusations, and continued to view the Russians as barbarians who had treated us inhumanely during the war. But, we were grateful for our freedom and forgave them for their words and past injustices. We made plans to leave Europe, hoping that our lives in another place would be better. And, they were.

After many years of living in different countries and continents in pursuit of a better life, I found myself with a young family of my own, living in a small suburb in New Jersey. I was surrounded by people of my own faith, no longer living among hostile, anti-semitic neighbors. I thought I had found my long-sought haven. To my dismay, however, I was once again in the unpopular minority. I was the only one with a foreign accent, the only one without an extended family, the only one whose parents did not come for the holidays and to school activities to beam with pride at their grandchildren. Although I tried to fit in, I was unsuccessful. With one exception, my neighbors did not ask me how I survived the war. They did not open their doors, did not include us, and did not make us feel welcome. Parties were planned for adults as well as children; we were excluded. We raised our children alone, keeping to ourselves, and socializing mostly with other survivors of World War II. I recently inquired of several friends with backgrounds similar to mine, and learned that their experiences in America were identical to mine.

It has taken many years for us to vocalize our thoughts and for others to listen. It has taken many years for Elie Wiesel to receive the Nobel Prize, for Stephen Spielberg to make his award-winning film about the Holocaust, and for survivors to earn respectability and social stature in their communities. Even today, after living in the same house on the same lovely suburban street for nearly 30 years, I am in many respects still a foreigner.

Today, as I listen to the radio, I play the "what if" game, and ask myself: What would have happened if Anne Frank had survived the war, and traveled to the United States as I did? How would her neighbors have received her? How would they have perceived her accent, her mannerisms? They may have considered her diary good reading materials, yet would they have welcomed her next door? I wonder, must a person die and become a martyr, published posthumously, in order to be accepted and respected by who live on her block?

Irene Frisch

Chapter 8
The Liberation of Drohobycz by the Soviets

As the tides of war turned against Germany, Drohobycz was bombed regularly by the Allies. One day, 300 American planes flew over and bombed the city in an attempt to destroy the oil refineries which supplied gas for the Germans. Huddled in Frania's apartment, we were terrified. We couldn't leave to seek shelter from the bombs because we might be recognized.

One night, the bombing was so terrible that the walls of the house shook and pulsed with each explosion. We took a huge chance and ventured outside. It was dark and no one recognized us. In the confusion, Irene was separated from us and became lost in the smoke and flames. She came across a house from which she heard voices. In a frantic attempt to find shelter, she went inside. When she was asked to identify herself, she replied that she had been visiting an aunt in the city and had been caught up in the bombing.

Irene during her visit to Drohobycz in front of the
house in which we lived after the war.

I went out as well and had a scare when a young man whom I didn't know followed me. I managed to lose him. When the bombing stopped my mother and I returned to Frania's apartment where we learned that Irene was missing. We were all frantic. Frania went out to search for her and found her by her voice in the home she had entered. Frania took her back home. The next day, Frania went out and when she came back she had wonderful news. She said she had seen Russian soldiers on the street and the Germans were gone!

My mother took us by the hand, two barefooted children (we had grown out of our shoes during our years in hiding) and we went out into the streets. We suddenly felt free. Naively, we felt safe. It was not a very wise thing to do because the Germans could easily come back at a moment's notice, as it often happens when the front lines are being recaptured. This had happened in the neighboring city of Sambor where my father's cousin, who was a physician, and his pregnant wife, had successfully remained hidden during the German occupation. They too emerged from their hiding place only to find that the Germans had temporarily returned. They were both murdered one day before the liberation by the Soviets.

My mother took Irene and me to our old neighborhood. As we walked barefoot down the street the people who had been our neighbors before the war watched us surreptitiously through the windows. They appeared to be very upset that we were still alive because we were living witnesses of what they had done to the Jews.

When we came to our old house we rang the bell. A Ukrainian man, an engineer, who had known my father before the war, answered the door. When he saw us, he became very frightened. The next day he moved out even though it wasn't necessary because we didn't want to move back in. We were afraid to stay alone. Instead, the few Jews from the area who had survived the war, moved into one apartment house together. We felt safer this way. We lived in two rooms on the first floor. My mother's younger sister, Tosia, came to live with us. Her husband, an accountant, and her son also survived.

Our new rooms had apparently originally been a store as it had a big display window at street level. We covered the windows with boxes to pre-serve our privacy. When we moved in the rooms were completely empty. Irene and I went out to look for

A drawing of Pola and Irene dragging a bed through the streets of Drohobycz after liberation. By Sam Arbiser.

beds. We found one bed but there was no one to help us carry it. So Irene and I—two barefoot, skinny girls—dragged it through the streets of Drohobycz. We had to stop every few minutes to rest. It took us nearly all day to get it home. Slowly we furnished the apartment with tables and chairs we found in the bombed-out houses.

In the early days, it was very difficult to get food. One day my mother heard that the Russians were distributing free bread in the street. She told me to go and get some, but I was ashamed to beg for bread. My mother told me, "If you do not go, we will not eat." So I went and got the bread. When I arrived at the place where they were distributing the bread, a young man thoughtfully threw me a loaf of bread over the heads of the waiting crowd.

In the beginning, in order to support us my mother sold baked cookies on the open market in the freezing cold as we had only four *zlotys* on the day of liberation. My mother's nose bled from the cold. One day a hunchbacked man approached her and asked if she would sell yeast he would provide for her. She agreed and it was a good move. The man eventually became very successful.

Later, my mother was able to open a small restaurant with her sister, Tosia. As the Russian soldiers returned to Russia from Germany they passed through the city and frequented my mother's restaurant. They paid for the food with different goods like fabrics and watches. Business was good. My mother was able to buy us shoes and even saved some money.

Frania was now working at a dairy products company. One day, she told me to meet her outside the company and she gave me milk and butter. She told me to sell it and go to the movies. I was very excited because I hadn't been to a movie in years. We were so hungry for any kind of entertainment that Irene and I would see the same movie many times.

One day I decided that I should get a job and help. In the city, there was a Russian casino for officers and they needed a waitress. I lied and told them that I was sixteen years old and they hired me. It was a good job because I got food, which I brought home. Everything was going fine until one day I was serving a group of Russian officers. One of them tried to touch my cheek and I went completely wild and threw all the food at him.

My employers decided I was a mental case and I could not work with other people, so they put me to work cutting bread. I was presented with thirty or forty loaves to cut with a single dull knife. Shortly, I had cut my hands badly so my employers assigned me to peel potatoes. I didn't do very well at that either. The sacks of potatoes were huge. The Russian soldiers felt sorry for me and helped me peel them. When my employers discovered this they finally lost their patience and fired me.

My mother's restaurant was doing fine but still there was not enough money for luxuries. In the apartment building where all the Jews lived, there were two families with boys about my age. I played cards with them for money—not too much, just change. I cheated and I won. With my ill-gotten gains, Irene, my cousin and I bought ice cream. Irene and my cousin were waiting for me in anticipation, pressing their faces against the window, when I emerged with my ill-gotten gains. When I smiled, they knew I had won and we all went for ice cream.

Occasionally in the evenings, I went to the park where there was an orchestra and dancing. My mother didn't know about it. I didn't know how to dance either but it was a real treat to see people dancing again.

When we were liberated, due to lack of vitamins, my eyes were badly affected. I had lost my eyelashes as well. My mother fed me milk and strawberries with sour cream and Napoleons. I didn't want to eat them, but she insisted, and my eyes slowly improved. In addition, after we emerged from hiding I could not speak above a whisper from the years of silence.

At the Russian school Irene and I now attended there were only a few Jewish students. I didn't have any relationship with the non-Jewish students because when the Germans occupied the town they had told me not to come to their home any more. Now, I no longer wished to have anything to do with them.

There was some excitement in our post-war lives. In our apartment house lived three Russian women: a mother and her two pretty daughters. The two girls regularly went to the movies with the Russian soldiers. When they asked me if I wanted to go I agreed happily. As it turned out, the tickets for that night's movie were all sold out, so one of the Russian soldiers took out a pistol and threatened the ticket taker with it until they let us in. The management even provided chairs for us to sit on!

In a more frightening incident, these same girls brought two Russian soldiers to our apartment. One of the soldiers tried to touch me and I kicked him. He took out a pistol to shoot me. He shouted at me "We liberated you and this is the way you treat me!" My mother came running from the kitchen and stood in front of me until they left.

DREAMS

We all have dreams. It has long been a dream of
mine to visit the house of my early childhood. The
last time I slept in that house was 1939. It was
the beginning of World War II. The Russian army
occupied our town in Poland, expelling us from our
house and from our community because of my parents'
affluence. When the Nazis later occupied our town,
they, too, moved into our large and comfortable
house. At the end of the war, we left Europe, never
to return to that house. Now, after many years and
moves to many countries, I have finally established a permanent residence and roots in the United
States. Yet, over the years, I have continued to
dream of my pre-war home, and to envy those people
who spend their entire lives in one place.

Since our retirement, my husband and I travel to
Europe often. When planning each trip, I consider
visiting my pre-war childhood home. The idea lin-
gers and grows and, I am embarrassed to admit, has
become a kind of obsession for me. A few years ago,
I made an unplanned stop in Poland while on vaca-

tion. Once there, I contacted some people from my hometown, hoping to arrange a visit. They advised me that a trip to my hometown—then a part of the Soviet Union—would be dangerous. Even so, I stood for hours in the office of the Russian Consulate, hoping to obtain a visa. When I was not issued one, I left, greatly disappointed.

Some time later, I received through some newly-made acquaintance a photograph of my childhood house. I studied the image before me. In my memory, the house is a modern, beautiful, custom-built one-family home surrounded by a lovely garden, professionally landscaped and watered daily by my mother. This photograph, taken recently, depicted a dilapidated building fronted by seven or eight mailboxes and, therefore, probably inhabited by as many families. The garden was no longer there. Yet, even the grim revelation that my childhood home does not exist in reality as it does in my memory has not deterred my hopes and nostalgia entirely. Are my stubborn dreams of returning to that home another manifestation of my unusual war-time experiences? Has my nostalgia for that pre-war home resulted from the brevity of my happy childhood, and from my numerous displacements during and after the war? I believed so until recently, when a strange incident led me to conclude that many of us secretly yearn to revisit our childhood homes.

On a hot afternoon in August, I took my aging dog for a walk on our quiet street in Teaneck, New Jersey. Upon our return, I spotted a large car parked in front of my house. A handsome, silver-haired gentleman sat in the driver's seat, pointing at the house and talking to the passengers of his car. I was certain they were looking for someone. As I approached the front walk, the gentleman rolled down his window and asked if I knew who lived in that house. He then explained that he lived in that house with his former wife and their four children some twenty-eight years ago. When I identified myself as the current owner, the gentleman and his passengers spilled out of the car. He introduced an elderly, nondescript woman as his current wife, and a young, attractive woman and her three children as his daughter and her children.

The daughter, a woman in her late thirties, spoke English with a lovely French accent, while her three children spoke no English at all. She told me that she had lived in our house for one year, as a child, that she missed it, that she often told her children about the house. Then, in a small, plaintive voice, she asked: "Can we come in?" How could I refuse? I invited the party in, introduced them to my bewildered husband, and gave them a quick tour.

I saw that the young woman was very emotional and had tears in her eyes. She spoke to her children in French, explaining to them the old sleeping arrangements and recounting some good memories and anecdotes from her early childhood. She also told me that she left the house, and the United States, at the age of 10, and had not returned to the States since then. She thanked me warmly for inviting her in, confiding that she had always dreamed of revisiting her childhood home but had never really believed it was possible. Although our childhood experiences differed greatly, I identified with her and confessed that I, too, often dream of returning to my childhood home.

After the group departed, I sat down and wondered at our shared feelings and longing for our child-hood homes. I also sorted through my few memories of the previous owners' one year in my house. We purchased this small, comfortable house in Teaneck from them some twenty-eight years ago. We could afford this house largely because the sellers—newly divorced—needed to sell their home quickly. Our new neighbors soon provided details about the previous owners: The wife was a college professor from Paris, and the husband a former American G.I. They had met and married while he was stationed in Paris during World War II. They remained in Europe for several years, had four children together, and later came to the States and purchased this home in Teaneck.

The beautiful, sophisticated French wife never adapted to the sleepy, suburban community. Unhappy with her American home and her marriage, she left her husband and returned to Paris with their four children, while her husband remained in the United States. Understandably, he was eager to dispose of the house as soon as possible, and accepted our low bid.

Our neighbors also informed us that the unfortunate couple lived in the house for only one year, and that during that time the unhappy wife showed no interest in the house, or in the neighborhood. The house certainly looked neglected, its rooms dirty and undecorated. This, too, probably contributed to the sellers' acceptance of our low bid.

Surely, the four children's brief year in the house must have been a strained, unhappy time, culminating in the divorce and their permanent separation from their father. Nonetheless the daughter has continued to cherish her memories from that brief period, and has yearned to return to this childhood home. Perhaps it is the fate of all people who are prematurely evicted from a childhood home, under circumstances beyond their control, to yearn for that home and for all it represents.

I was glad to have helped the daughter attain her dream, but sad at the thought that I would never achieve my own dream. Recent political changes in Eastern Europe bar my return to my childhood home

which, according to the current photograph in my
possession, no longer exists in the condition etched
in my memory. This dream of mine is better left
unrealized.

September, 1995
Irene Frisch

Chapter 9
Leaving Drohobycz

After the war, Drohobycz remained in the Ukraine. When we discovered that we, as ex-Polish citizens, had the right to return to the newly-reconstituted post-war Poland, we decided to leave Drohobycz. Before our departure, Frania and my mother prepared a stockpile of noodles and dried cakes for the journey, which they put into pillowcases. We also acquired potatoes and onions for the journey.

My mother, Frania, Irene and I left Drohobycz for the last time on a freight train. My aunt and her husband and son also went with us. It was cold and in the middle of the car there was an iron stove for heating and cooking. On both sides of the wagon there were bunk beds where we slept. We traveled for six weeks through a destroyed Europe. There were no homes or businesses, just rubble. There was nothing to eat and little fresh water to drink. At the railroad stations, there were stands of drinking

My father, Israel, after liberation.

water, which were staffed by Polish women but when they saw Jews they became very unpleasant. I began to write a diary describing what I saw on the train.

In the meantime, unknown to us, my father had miraculously survived many concentration and labor camps including Plaszow, Wieliczka (a salt mine), Madjanek, and Auschwitz and finally Flossenberg. While in a cattle car going to Auschwitz, my father and his friend, Mr. Selinger, opened the door intending to jump into the river when crossing a bridge at their first opportunity. They abandoned this idea quickly because if the Germans didn't kill them, the locals would. The Poles hated the Jews as much as the Germans and besides they wanted to get rid of the witnesses to their deeds.

After my father had been liberated in Flossenburg in Bavaria he kissed the boots of the first American soldier that he saw. After he recovered, he set off east to Krakow in search of us. As he traveled through Poland, at various stops he encountered the

Polish Red Cross. He was treated very unpleasantly when they found out he was a Jew.

In Krakow a Jewish organization had established a meeting place where Jewish survivors could write their names in hopes of finding their relatives and friends. My father met another man from Drohobycz and from him he discovered that we had survived. The man gave him the number of the train on which we had just departed. My father followed the man's instructions and one day, there came a knock on the train door. We slid open the heavy door and there was my father! It was an indescribable feeling to see him again. We had thought that he was dead, but here he stood with a smile on his face. Unbelievable! It was only in our dreams. We were again a family.

Considering everything, he didn't look too bad. The Germans had knocked out all of his teeth during his stay in the camps. After he was liberated the American Army made him mayor of the city of Flossenberg. In that capacity, he had plenty to eat and good clothing. They also helped him to replace his teeth.

After traveling for a few weeks, we stopped at Legnica, the 'City of Gardens,' where we found some intact homes. We got an apartment as a family and another smaller one for Frania in the same house. My parents made a living by opening a dry-goods store in the space below our apartment. Later, my father opened the first fur store in Legnica and hired two people to sew for him. In Legnica, there were only a few Jews left and we were surrounded by Polish antisemites.

In Legnica, my parents were afraid to send us to school so we were schooled at home. First we had a German teacher who had taught biology in high school during the 1930s. She also taught me piano. Apparently, she didn't know we were Jewish because one day she brought a biology book she had written that detailed the differences between the 'Aryans' and the Jews and described how 'Aryans' were a superior race and Jews were a menace. When my father saw the book, he fired her on the spot.

Our next teachers were a brother and sister. The brother's specialty was chemistry and he taught me chemistry, physics, and math. His sister taught me literature and history. They were both very good teachers. The brother introduced me to chemistry in such an interesting way that I grew to like it very much and eventually I made it part of my profession.

Pola, Irene and their father in Frankfurt, Germany in 1960

Chapter 10
We Leave Poland for Israel

Eventually my parents decided they didn't want to stay in Poland any longer and would go to Israel. So we went to the border city of Klodzko to get the papers required to leave Poland. We ended up spending a year there waiting for permission to leave. We never did receive the papers so we returned to Legnica, where we finally got the papers to go to Israel.

During this time, Frania lived with us. We wanted to take Frania to Israel with us but she was afraid to go and decided to stay in Poland. We left everything for her: our apartment and furnishings. In the taxi Irene and I took Frania's wedding ring from her finger and replaced it with a much heavier and nicer ring of my parent's. They never knew we had done it. It was very hard to say goodbye to Frania: we didn't know if we would ever see her again. Our lives had been so entangled together.

We all cried as we said goodbye, never to see her again!

We traveled from Legnica to the port of Gdynia by train. When our train stopped in Breslau (Wroclaw), our luggage was thoroughly searched for twenty-four hours by secret police, who were once acquaintances of my father and who hoped to find some money. They did not and we finally left Poland.

Chapter 11
Our Life in Israel

We left Poland for Israel on an old dilapidated boat. The journey lasted six weeks, during which we were all very seasick—my mother the worst of all. It was a long, hard journey in barely adequate conditions. There was no privacy at all. There were many people on the boat and sanitary conditions were almost non-existent. Everyone slept and ate together. We sailed through the Baltic Sea, the English Channel, the Atlantic Ocean, the Straits of Gibraltar, and into the Mediterranean Sea and finally arrived at Haifa in Israel.

Upon arrival in the port of Haifa all of us were shocked. Everything and everyone was Jewish! The people, the soldiers, everyone! The longshoremen who unloaded the boat were Jews from Salonika, Greece. When we disembarked from the boat, we all went into a small shop and we were introduced to *Leben*, a drink similar to yogurt but which is prepared differently. To celebrate our arrival, my father bought everyone a drink.

All the people from the boat were transferred onto trucks. After a short trip in the dark we stopped in an unknown place. We unloaded our things in the dark and sat on our luggage. In the morning, we discovered that we were in a tent without walls. Later, the refugees were assigned to barracks in a refugee camp called *Shar Aliyah* that was located in a suburb of Haifa.

My family was assigned a barrack with three other families. Each family got one corner of their own. There was a shower, but the water was cold. The food was served in shifts in a central area of the camp at long tables and people of different cultures sat together at the same table. Big tureens of soup were placed on the tables. One woman, a Yemeni, took the whole tureen and began to eat it all herself because she didn't know otherwise.

The camp was a transition step before we were divided into different settlements or other camps. We had few possessions. Many people had no shoes, and when it rained the husbands carried the women on their backs, like sacks of potatoes. Everyone was very polite but it was not an easy time.

The camp had a fence around it that was manned by special guards. One day, my sister and myself decided to leave the camp to see Haifa without telling our parents. We slid under the fence and boarded a bus. We didn't know the language or where to go. The bus driver asked us in Hebrew where we wanted to go. I said *"Zwei Przystankes"* ('two stops'). He realized that we had escaped from the camp, so he called the camp police and they retrieved us.

The camp police questioned Irene and me about our destination. The police were young men, one of whom was tall and blond, the other dark. The interrogation quickly changed into a pleasant conversation. They asked Irene and me if we would like to go out with them on a date. Since we were eager for a change of scenery,we agreed and they came to our barracks and took us out. We went to a very nice bar on Mt. Carmel where they bought us drinks and we danced. Then we returned. It was a pleasant experience.

We stayed at *Shar Aliyah* for a few weeks then my parents discovered that my mother's niece, the daughter of her oldest brother, Hershel, lived in a suburb of Tel Aviv with her husband and three children. They invited us to stay with them until we found a place of our own. After a few weeks my parents were able to rent an apartment on a street called *Yonah Hanavi* near Mugrabi, close to the center of Tel Aviv. We were ecstatic!

Tel Aviv was bursting with life, full of excitement. We called it a 'small Paris.' Our lives started to normalize. My sister got a job in a bookstore and I started working in a pharmacy, although I did not know how to speak Hebrew. Irene eventually went to *Ulpan* to learn Hebrew and later she was drafted into the Israeli army. After six weeks of boot camp she was assigned to the headquarters of General Yitzak Rabin, the future prime minister of Israel.

My mother was devastated when my sister entered the army. A woman in the army! My sister loved chocolate cake so my mother made her a cake. Her method of delivery was unorthodox: she stopped all military men she found in the streets of Tel Aviv and asked in Yiddish whether he was in the same camp with my sister. Eventually, she found one officer who was based at Irene's camp and he delivered the cake to her.

Irene in the Israeli army in the early 1950s

My father had a very hard time adjusting to life in Israel, largely because of his inability to make a living. Furs were not needed in Israel and there was no market for luxury goods. He got very depressed and decided to return to Germany. My Uncle Mano had also returned to Germany after the war as had a few of the surviving relatives of my mother. My father made contact with a man named Mr. Fisher, who helped him to re-establish himself in Germany. My father got a very nice apartment and settled down again.

Meantime, I decided to return to school at the Hebrew University in Jerusalem. My knowledge of Hebrew was very limited, so Irene, who was fluent in the language, journeyed to Jerusalem and pretended to be me when speaking to the administration. I was accepted and shortly thereafter I started in the Department of Medical Science. At this time my mother and Irene went to visit my father in Germany.

The professors at Hebrew University were very kind and patient with their students who came from all over the world and spoke many different languages. Irene spoke Hebrew much better than me because she had been to *Ulpan* (a school for learning the Hebrew language) and had a talent for languages. During my first exam in chemistry, I couldn't remember some Hebrew words so I used Polish words. Two days later Dr. Kaczalsky (who later changed his name to 'Kazir' and became President of Israel) called me in and informed me that I was very lucky he understood Polish.

During my first days in Jerusalem, I met two girls from Poland: Paula and Maryla, with whom I shared rooms and food. We lived, ate, and studied together until graduation. Sometimes, when we had only enough money to invest in either a meal or a movie, we chose the movie. Afterwards, we were hungry so we crashed weddings where we ate very well. No one ever asked us who we were.

Another friend in Jerusalem was Dov, who was a medical student. Of his entire family, he alone had survived the war and had come to Israel. While he was in medical school he lived in a hotel and worked there as a night watchman in exchange for his room. To sustain himself he delivered newspapers for pocket change at six in the morning. He was so skinny that his ears stuck out—the *sabras* called him "Dov with Big Ears." Later, he got a job in the medical school itself. He lived not far from us and when we came from Tel Aviv with packages of food, we always called him and asked him to eat with us. Dov finished and became very successful.

My advisor was Professor Olitzki. He was from Germany and was head of the department. As part of the university studies, each student had to give a seminar on a certain subject. I knew the subjects, but I had a limited knowledge of Hebrew and English. Some people in my department helped me. They translated my work from English to Hebrew. One read it to me aloud and I wrote it phonetically in Latin letters. I wrote from left to right unlike in Hebrew, which goes from right to left. My advisor, Professor Olitzki, suspected something was not right because of the way I turned the pages and while I was talking he began to edge toward me. I closed my notes so he could not see them. After the seminar, Professor Olitzki called me to his office and asked me what was really going on and I admitted what I had done. I graduated from Hebrew University in 1957 with a master's degree in Medical Science with an emphasis on microbiology and biochemistry.

Pola with her diploma
from Hebrew University.

Pola at her graduation ceremony
from Hebrew University. David Ben-
Gurion, the first prime minister
of Israel, is sitting in the far
left corner.

Professor Olitzki went with me to my first job interview. Few people had cars in those days so we went by bus from Jerusalem to Tel Hashomer Hospital. The journey required two buses from Jerusalem to Tel Aviv and then from Tel Aviv to Tel Hashomer Hospital where he introduced me as his student. I will never forget how he treated me. As a wedding present, he gave me a week off and assigned other people to continue my experiment.

One day in Tel Aviv I was sitting with my mother in the coffeehouse on Mugrabi Square when two young men came in. I knew one of them, Josef, from Poland and he waved to me from afar. Josef and his friend sat at another table with their coffees. Evidently, the other young man asked Josef to introduce him to me but both were too shy to stop at our table. They lived in Haifa and were mechanical engineers.

They wrote me a letter informing me that Josef would be in Tel Aviv next Saturday and he would like to meet me near the pharmacy where I used to work. However, their plan was that Josef would not come to the meeting, pleading sickness and instead the other man would come. What Josef didn't know was that I was living in Jerusalem where I was attending Hebrew Uni-

Sam in an Israeli
commando unit.

Sam at work at the Vulcan
plant. He is standing in
front of a radial drill
press.

Pola and Sam's wedding picture.

versity and the letter didn't reach me. The other man was Sam Arbiser, my future husband.

Sam kept the appointment as planned and nobody came. But he was persistent. Next week both of them came to my house in Tel Aviv. My mother was in Germany at this time and Irene and I were cleaning the apartment. We stopped cleaning, changed our clothes, and made some food. Sam, when offered a sandwich, refused because he was shy. However, after watching us eat for awhile, he asked if he could have one too.

Sam and I dated for one year. I wrote to my parents that I had met someone and wished to get married. Two days later my mother showed up in Tel Aviv in a bit of a panic. Sam and I were married in a small wedding at a rabbi's house with just my parents, Sam's brother, Nathan (who had survived the war with Sam in Siberia), Nathan's wife, Frieda, and Sam's aunt were in attendance. Sam's parents, sister, and brother and entire family had been murdered in the death camp of Treblinka outside Warsaw. To our sorrow, Frania, living in Poland, was unable to attend.

I had to finish my studies so I stayed in Jerusalem while Sam stayed in Haifa were he was the head of the machine building department at Vulcan, the largest foundry in the Middle East. He also served in the reserves. Everyone in Israel, male and female, had to serve either in the regular or reserve army. We met on the weekends in Tel Aviv at my mother's apartment. This continued for two years. My friends, Paula and Maryla, also married at approximately the same time as did Sam and me and our husbands became good friends. We didn't have much money, but in the evenings we went out to dinner or to the movies. Once a week, each couple had the others over to their home for coffee and conversation.

My father helped Sam and I get and furnish a beautiful apartment near *Kikar Dizengof*, a square in Tel Aviv. My mother alternated between living with us in Israel and in Germany with my father. My mother and Sam had a very nice relationship. He always brought her chocolates and took her to coffee-houses. Once, when he went to Germany to visit my mother who was very sick, Sam asked me what she would like him to bring her. My mother wanted a watermelon, so Sam carried a watermelon on the airplane all the way from Tel Aviv to Frankfurt, Germany.

In 1956, my mother became ill. She had diabetes and had also never really recovered from the death of my brother, Ludwik. Irene wrote me a letter about my mother's condition. I immediately took a leave of absence from my work in the hospital after explaining why, and went to Frankfurt. When I arrived, my mother looked terrible. She was 58 years old but she looked like she was 80. I

Sara Bienstock at age 57 or 58.

stayed with her in Frankfurt, hoping she would improve.

One day Irene and I took my mother for a checkup at the hospital at Heidelberg University, where Irene attended medical school. Irene brought my mother a book to read, *Bonjour Tristesse* by Francois Sagan. The next day, around six in the morning, I got a call from the hospital. I was told that my mother was unconscious. My father, my mother's sister, Tosia, and myself drove to Heidelberg. My mother had had a stroke and after a few hours she passed away.

According to the clinic's rules, you had to donate your body to the University for research, but this was against our Jewish beliefs. My father commandeered an ambulance and we smuggled my mother's body out of the hospital. With my deceased mother's body in the back we drove to Frankfurt. It was Friday morning and the funeral had to be the same day (before Sabbath) according to Jewish law. We called from Heidelberg and made arrangements ahead of time, so the *chevra kaddisha* (burial society) was waiting for us. We buried my mother in the Frankfurt cemetery on May 13, 1957.

Sam also visited my mother in Frankfurt during her illness, but he could not stay indefinitely as he had a job in Israel in the factory of Hamat, where he was a chief engineer. He had achieved the highest position possible in his field at an early age.

After my mother's death I returned to Israel. I thought my job as a bacteriologist at Tel Hashomer Hospital was secure because when I left for Germany to be with my mother my boss had promised me he would keep my job for me. Unfortunately, in the meantime, an American physician's wife had been given my job. I was very upset and immediately began to look for another job. It wasn't easy as there were many educated people in Israel. Sometimes jobs didn't open up until someone retired or died.

After returning from Germany, I was very lonely and grieving the loss of my mother. With nothing to do, I just stayed in my room. I needed to be occupied as all my life I had either studied or worked. I was desperate to get a job. One day I applied at a research institute called the Professor Felix Institute in Abu Kabir, a suburb of Tel Aviv, that was headed by Dr. Ilan. During the interview, he said they had an opening but no money for a salary. I said I would start the next day and he could pay me when he could. He agreed. At the end of the month, I got my first paycheck and it was very generous.

My life in Israel had a very important influence on my self esteem. I regained my self assurance which I lost during the German occupation and by the antisemitic experiences during the war.

While we were in Israel, we were continuously in touch with Frania. We sent her packages and money so she wouldn't have to work. What we did was nothing special—she had risked her life for us. When I wrote her that I was getting married, she wrote me a very unusual letter. She replied: "Your husband, doesn't know me, and he doesn't have the same feelings towards me, so he may object to you sending me money. If this is the case, please stop sending it. I don't want you to have any problems." But Sam never objected, in fact, he sometimes reminded me when it was time to do so.

Chapter 12
We Emigrate to the United States

We had been in Israel for ten years, but Sam was restless and wanted to see the world. I, on the other hand, loved Israel and my friends. When Sam was invited by a company in Chicago in the United States to work for them, I was very upset but agreed to go with him. We got our papers in six weeks because his profession had preference in the United States. We sold our beautiful furniture and gave up our wonderful apartment, which was the first place we had lived together. When the movers came to pick up the furniture, I locked myself in the bathroom and cried inconsolably.

Before leaving Israel we sold most of our possessions and transferred the money to my father in Frankfurt am Main. Sam and I left Israel by boat from Haifa. Sam's brother, Nathan, and his wife, Frieda, gave us a ride in their car to the port and waited until the boat departed. In Naples, we landed with just a few dollars in our possession. My father wired us some money so we could pay the zero star hotel, the *Pensione Azura*.

Prior to getting the money from my father we went out to dinner. We sought out a restaurant off the tourist path. We checked out which streets had cobble-stones and went down one of those. We found a little restaurant that was situated on both sides of the street. One side had the kitchen and the other was the dining room. They brought the food across the street. We had a five-course dinner for one dollar each. As we ate, a street peddler came by and tried to sell us some jewelry. The owner of the restaurant cautioned us with his finger in a "No, no!" gesture not to deal with him.

Finally, in December 1960, we took the liner *S.S. United States*, the finest ship in the world, from Bremerhaven, Germany to the United States. The weather was stormy and I was terribly seasick again as were most of the passengers on the boat. Only Sam was not sick—he sat alone in the restaurant having a good time. Fortunately, it took us only four days to cross the Atlantic. On the boat, we met several Jewish couples returning from Israel to the United

States and we tried to discover as much as possible about life in the United States.

We arrived in New York in December 1960. Sam had relatives in the United States—cousins on his father's side—and they came to meet us at the boat. Another cousin from Atlanta also came to New York to greet us at the pier.

We had to go through customs. We had in our possession a typewriter, on which we were not sure if we owed duty. The customs agent, who was heavily-built and blond, looked disagreeable. Sam wanted to avoid him but he could not. He looked over our passports and saw that we were coming from Israel. He became very friendly to us. He asked us if we knew his cousin in Tel Aviv, Mr. Rozensweig. He told us we had nothing to declare and waved us through.

We stayed with another cousin of Sam's who lived in New Jersey for a few days. Then Sam went to Chicago to settle down, find an apartment and buy a car. I was invited by my husband's cousin in Atlanta to come and stay with them for a few days. I arrived in Atlanta in December where it was still green and warm. The people were very polite and kind. As I walked along the road, several people stopped their cars and asked me if I wanted a ride. A policeman even asked me as I walked whether I needed any help. I loved Atlanta immediately and the southern people stole my heart.

Meantime, Sam went to his new job in Chicago. It was very, very cold. Sam's English was extremely limited and he had trouble with the public transportation system. Luckily, some Polish women were on the same bus with him and they helped him determine when to get off the bus. The owner of the foundry where Sam had to work showed Sam around his impressive plant. They agreed that Sam would start work next week so that he had time to rent an apartment and buy a car.

We had friends who lived in Chicago. They had come to the United States a year or two ahead of us. I had gone to Hebrew University with the woman who, like me, was a microbiologist. Her husband had finished medical school in Jerusalem. In Chicago, they rented a small apartment and had a baby boy. The apartment was not very nice and it was necessary to climb many stairs to get to it. They had lived better in Israel where their apartment had been beautiful, sunny and large. What Sam saw now was very depressing. To make matters worse, they told him that another friend, Marek, who was a chemical engineer had even worse living conditions. Sam began to worry about living conditions in the United States and whether he would be able to afford any decent housing.

Sam began to despair and questioned his wisdom about coming to the United States. One evening I called Sam and asked him how Chicago was and about our friends. He couldn't speak truthfully because they were in the same room with him. He answered they were like 'Alex in Frankfurt.' Alex was a perpetual student who lived in very poor circumstances. I said "Why don't you come and see Atlanta, it's very beautiful here." Sam was eager to come.

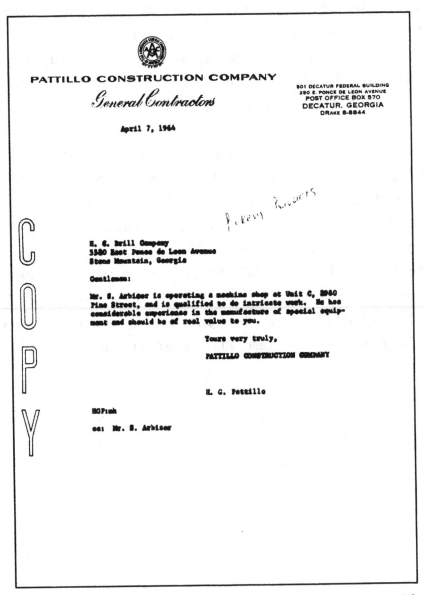

A copy of the letter Mr. Patillo sent out on behalf
of Sam's fledgling machine-building business in 1964.

Chapter 13
Life in Atlanta

Sam liked Atlanta too. My cousin, Helen, drove him to the Chamber of Commerce where he explained his situation. They asked if the company in Chicago had paid for his coming here. Sam said "No, we paid it ourselves." Thus it was determined that Sam did not have any contract with them. They said he didn't have to work for them and arranged a meeting with the owner of a company that built textile machinery, Meadows Manufacturing Company in Atlanta. Sam talked to his employer in Chicago and he was released from his agreement. Sam went to work for Meadows Manufacturing Company. He was the second salaried man after the owner. They liked him very much. Because of Sam's limited knowledge of English and Mr. Meadow's basic knowledge of drawing, Sam had to create models made of play doh that his boss liked very much.

I also started to look for work. Originally, I applied to Lays Potato Chips for a position as a chemist in their lab. When I arrived for the interview a man checked my credentials, which were probably better than his, and told me that they had a position open. However, the other employees were all men and he felt that a woman would create an unhealthy situation. I argued with him that I had come from a country where both men and women served in the army and I would not create any problems but it did no good. He also inferred that Sam would be jealous because they routinely scheduled meetings in the evenings. I told him, "If I wanted to have an affair I wouldn't have it here in your lab."

I wanted to work for the Center for Disease Control (CDC) but it is a federal agency and the first question on the application is "Are you a citizen of the United States?" I wasn't so I applied to Emory University since it is a private institution and had no such rules. I was interviewed by Dr. Tom Sellers whose specialty is infectious diseases. The interview was very simple because of language difficulties but he accepted me. However, I had to take a pay cut. At the CDC I would have made five times as much.

When I started to work at Emory University, Dr. Sellers gave me my own lab. I asked for one week to get the lab in order. I cleaned it from the floor to the ceiling. Then I gave him a list of needed equipment, which I got and we started a project which was connected with infectious diseases at Grady Hospital. Dr. Sellers needed grants to support his project, so he wrote to Washington, D.C. and a commission came to see what we were doing. When the gentleman arrived, Dr. Seller's asked me, "Pola, please explain what we are doing." I tried very hard, but I was worried about the future of the project because my English was poor. After he left, Dr. Seller's told me that the man from Washington had liked both the project and my English!

As I said before, southern people were very warm-hearted. We could not afford a car and one friend of ours, Ron Stephens, who worked at the same company as Sam, drove us both to work early each morning.

Dr. Seller's suggested that I read trashy paperback books to familiarize myself with English, but for which I would not have to check the dictionary all the time. I started reading a book called *The Apartment* and found that I understood most of it. Then I came upon a Russian name, which confused me because this was an American novel and had no Russian characters. I asked many people about the unfamiliar word. Dr. Seller's finally asked me to show him the word in the book. The word was an American profanity, which I taken to be a Russian proper name. When I showed it to him he exploded into laughter. In your native language, you learn bad words as a child, but I didn't know them in English.

Elizabeth Bauer, who had fled Germany before Hitler came to power, helped me as well. She explained things to me in German whenever I got in a bind. She showed me where to shop and accepted me as a friend. Together we went to the Atlanta Municipal Mart and my colleagues often took me home with my packages. My later experiences with other people were not always as pleasant.

In the first weeks in Atlanta, Sam passed his driver's test and we bought a new Chevrolet Impala for $2,415 in cash. This was a very important event in our lives. I had had to learn about American money. At first I didn't know the difference between a nickel and a dime and we knew nothing about credit and credit cards. According to our background, if you didn't have money you didn't buy it. We were told that paying cash was not smart because we would never get a credit history. This was not the only secret that we learned about American life.

Later, we discovered life insurance and social security. Three months after I started work, I was called into the office at Emory University and they advised me to buy life insurance. I was still young and inexperienced and asked them why I needed it. They explained that funerals in the United States were very expensive and if I loved my husband, I should buy life insurance. My answer was, "If I die now, let him pay." I did buy life insurance later.

We rented an apartment on Briarcliff Road, which was very convenient to Emory University. In the evenings we walked to Emory for English courses for foreign professionals. By that time, we had one car and Sam dropped me off one hour before starting time at my lab so he could get to work across town on time himself.

I worked for Dr. Sellers for over a year. I phage-typed staph infections in Grady Hospital. On the material I collected from the patients there was the notation "stump." I thought it was a last name and I wrote "Stump 1, Stump 2, Stump 3." I commented to

Dr. Seller's on how popular the name 'Stump' was in the United States. He laughed and explained that it meant the part of the limb left after amputation.

Atlanta was beautiful and my place of work was not far from downtown. I often went downtown by Davisons and watched the people pass by. It was a peculiar feeling because I felt like a stranger: I knew no one. After one year of working for Dr. Sellers, I applied for a Ph.D. program at Emory University. I was accepted with a full scholarship and they gave me $200 a month for books. My English was still not good and I made friends with medical students who were taking similar subjects. At this time, there were only two other females in the class. One of my professors, Dr. Brinkley, who was a professor of biochemistry, was quite a character. Sometimes in the evening instead of lecturing he would announce, "How about having a beer. I don't care to lecture now." Whenever that happened I called my husband and sister (who was visiting) and they came and we went and had a beer.

Once we had a test on which there was a question about methods. The question used the word 'enable' and I thought it meant 'unable' and I wrote the answer in that mode. My advisor, Dr. Tiger, called me to his office and asked me "Do you know what 'enable' means?" "Yes," I answered, "It means unable." He said no, it means "able." This is how I learned the English language—it was an adventure.

While I was studying at Emory University, we decided to buy a house and we found one in the area. We didn't know what we were doing but as my mother said, "The Good Lord goes with stupid people." We found a wonderful house in an area with good schools in the vicinity of Emory University. We still live there today.

When I was pregnant with Jack, the wife of my pediatrician, Dr. Herbert Alperin, who was my husband's cousin, gave me a baby shower. I didn't know about baby showers until I came to America and was working at Emory University, where there were many showers. I got all dressed up and arrived at the shower. Everybody was wearing shorts, so next time I wore shorts and everybody was dressed formally. Someone explained to me that before you go you have to ask what kind of shower it is.

Jack, my son, was born in 1962. When Jack was one year old, Sam opened an engineering business of his own, the Arbiser Machine Building Company. For years, Sam had dreamed of having his own business. While he was working for Meadows, from our savings we bought several machines from government auctions which we installed in our carport. Working in his free time, Sam got a few customers and saved a small amount of money. One day Sam came home and said, "I quit my job." We had $600 to keep us alive.

We rented a space from Patillo Construction Company. The space was small and there was a small office attached. Mr. Patillo brought us the lease and told Sam that since he was just starting, he would reduce the monthly payments for the first three months. I came to the office everyday with Jack. There was no furniture, so we sat on the floor on a blanket. The only thing in the office was a telephone. Nevertheless, it was a very exciting time for both of us.

It was hard for Sam because he had no connections in the United States in his field. He worked until noon and then put on a tie and became a salesman, visiting different companies to solicit business. A few days after we opened the business, Mr. Patillo came to visit and he asked Sam how he was doing. Sam replied, "Not bad, but I could use more work—I need connections." The next day Mr. Patillo mailed us copies of a stack of letters that he had sent to his tenants and friends in the business world. Mr. Patillo owned many industrial sites. Sam visited the ones that had gotten Mr. Patillo's letter and got work. Mr. Patillo was a kind man and expected nothing in return. He was our 'incidental meeting' in Atlanta.

Mr. Patillo was the first person to invite Sam and myself to dinner. He treated us wonderfully. He invited Sam to meetings at the Chamber of Commerce, where he introduced him and explained what he did. He recommended him highly. He also invited Sam to meetings with people in high positions in Atlanta city government and Georgia state government, where he praised him professionally and personally. These contacts created additional work for our company. We remain in touch with Mr. Patillo until today. We have dinners together and know his beautiful family.

Whenever Sam needed advice he called Mr. Patillo and asked him. The business developed nicely and we decided to construct our own building but we had no experience in how to go about it. Mr. Patillo helped us again. He offered to build it for us, without any papers at all—just on a handshake. Later, he helped us get a loan from the bank and he sold us the land.

Our daughter, Sherry, was born in 1964. I didn't know how to deal with the children. When Jack was a baby, he got the hiccups and I got very frightened. Dr. Alperin was very helpful. He always answered my naive questions without laughing at me.

By the time Sherry was born I had started working with Sam a little bit more, so I needed help at home. Maggie Reese, who had advertised in the paper, came to work for me. She worked for our family for over twenty years. She taught me many things about child rearing. She took extremely good care of my children. I am still in touch with Maggie today.

During this time, my father lived in Germany, but he frequently came to visit us in the United States. Eventually, he decided to move to the United States as well. He needed surgery, which he could receive here. My father loved fishing and he taught Sam this hobby. He stayed with us, but he was not very happy. He couldn't speak English to my children,

My father, Israel, fishing
in Scotland.

Israel Bienstock with
Sherry, Pola's daughter,
during one of his visits to
the United States.

169

read the newspaper, or watch television. In Europe he could walk to coffeehouses and meet his friends.

I was in school at Emory University at the time and every day I took him with me and left him by a lake in a park near the home of the President of Emory University. He fished all day and I came to see him for lunch. Most of the time he was alone, and he was not happy. He said "Take an old tree and transplant it, it will not catch." After awhile, he returned to Europe. While there he had a heart attack and passed away in Frankfurt. My husband and my sister went to Germany for the funeral and he is buried in Frankfurt next to my mother. I was very sad but felt I had to stay home with my children. When I was sitting *shivah* (mourning), Rabbi Feldman from Beth Jacob synagogue came to our house. We were new members of Beth Jacob, and I don't know how he found out about my father's death. I have always appreciated his *mitzvah*.

One time, Jack came home from kindergarten crying. He asked me, "How come all the children in my class have several grandparents, but I have only one?" My children never met any of their grandparents, except for my father. My mother had already passed away before they were born and Sam's entire family with the exception of his brother, Nathan, had all perished in the Treblinka death camp. It was hard for me to explain to a five-year-old child why he was largely without grandparents. My father did come to visit us occasionally from Europe and he showed them the tatooed number from the camps on his arm. Sam and I are very grateful for our grandchildren. We thank God every day that our children live here in Atlanta because when we came here, we were often lonely, especially during the holidays.

When my children started elementary school, I studied the English language, American history, and geography with them, which helped me a great deal. I also volunteered at the school once a week. Both our children knew how to read and write when they started school. They also knew their multiplication tables because Sam played a game with them. While we ate dinner, we played a math game that involved multiplication. When we traveled we played games with them involving which state the cars on the road came from and this helped with their geography.

Once my son, Jack, came home from school (his fellow students called him "Brain") and announced that one of his friends had gotten a demerit. I didn't know what that meant, so I said "Jack, you are a good student, why didn't you get one?" My son laughed and explained.

Once at home I got an obscene phone call. I didn't understand what the man was saying and asked him politely to repeat it. He did so but I still didn't understand. I asked him to repeat it again. He got mad at me and hung up! Later, my children told me what the man had been trying to tell me and collapsed laughing.

Sherry was a very artistic child and inherited many qualities from Sam. She always helped her father do things like repair the lawn mower while Jack hid behind a book. She was a very good tennis player, was captain of her tennis team in high school, and was a cheerleader.

Many people thought that because I had an accent or couldn't speak well that I was illiterate. One family on my street had a daughter the same age as Sherry. Sherry came home one night very upset: the parents of her friend had forbidden their child to play with her because they were afraid their child might pick up "bad language habits" from me.

172

My children, after finishing elementary school, went to a very good public high school. Most of the children who attended the school had parents who were associated with Emory University. They also had very good teachers, with whom we stayed in constant touch. We never missed a PTA meeting.

We were very pleased when Jack and Sherry decided to go to Emory University. Jack decided to take pre-med. Sam was not happy, because he wanted Jack to go to Georgia Tech and follow him in practicing engineering as had three generations before him. During summer vacations, Jack worked for his father who paid him double and tried to make the work pleasant, hoping he would change his mind. But it didn't work. Upon returning home from work with Sam, he read my chemistry books.

When Jack was ten, Sam took him to a customer for whom we were building equipment for a lab. As he passed one room, Jack glanced in the door and saw a man writing a formula on the board. He identified it as an alcohol. The amazed man called him in and asked him how he knew that. Jack explained and the man invited Jack to talk with him about chemistry. As a result, Jack left the company loaded with glass flasks for his chemistry work. Jack wasn't interested in machinery building. Eventually, we accepted his decision and he began his pre-medical training. He loved chemistry and he finished his Bachelors and Masters degree in four years in chemistry at age twenty-one, *summa cum laude*.

Jack applied to several different medical schools. One day I received a notice that there was a registered letter waiting for him at the main post office in Decatur from the medical school in Augusta, Georgia. The next day, Jack was to go to Boston for an interview at Harvard University. It was just minutes before five in the evening when the post office closed for the day. Jack said he would feel so much better if he knew he had been accepted somewhere.

I was washing my hair, so I put a towel around my head and drove him to the post office in Decatur. The post office was already closed. Jack knocked on the door, and a man came and told him to come back tomorrow. So, I got out of the car, with the towel on my head and I said, "This is an emergency, open up!" I told him I needed the letter tonight. The man fetched the letter and when he looked at it he said "I understand why you wanted it." The letter said that Jack had been accepted and Jack was pleased that when he went to interview at Harvard he was already accepted elsewhere.

Jack's interview at Harvard was conducted by two people: a psychologist and an academic. The academic interviewed him first about his scholarly achievements. His only question was, "Why do you have a 'B' in Badminton?" This was the only 'B' Jack had ever gotten. The psychologist asked him if he considered himself to be a modest person. Jack replied, "Whatever I will say will be against me, but my mother thinks that I am a nice guy." He was accepted to Harvard and he went to medical school there.

Sherry started at Emory University three years after Jack. She majored in psychology. She was a very sweet, very pretty child. We called her "goody goody." Sherry finished her first four years at Emory University and went on to study art where she got a degree in Interior Design. She is very successful.

Jack had hobbies that helped him in school: collecting coins and an interest in minerals. Also we got interested in this hobby and devoted many weekends traveling to North Georgia and the Carolinas equipped with the proper tools for digging and panning. Sometimes we were successful finding gold dust or precious rocks. Jack's interest in minerals helped him in chemistry. Collecting coins helped him as well in his knowledge in geography and history: you had to know where the coin came from and the rulers at the time. Even today, as a married man with three children, Jack still collects rocks, minerals, and coins.

My children often came home with their friends and invited them to Jewish holidays at our home. Our children married six months apart. First, Sherry married Lee Bagel, a lawyer, and they have four beautiful children. Then Jack married a young lady, Zoya, whom he met in Boston. She attended Wellesley College. Jack called and said he was bringing a friend for the Passover. I asked who it was and he said it was a girl. Then I knew it was serious. We had been planning to go to our friends for Passover, but when I explained to them that Jack was bringing a girl home, we decided to hold it at our home. Zoya, his wife, is very nice young woman and is also a physician. Zoya was a student at Boston University Medical School and she did her

residency at Emory University Hospital. She prac-
tices here in Atlanta as a pathologist.

Jack graduated from Harvard University with both a
MD and Ph.D. He joined the staff of the Dermatology
Department at Emory University and conducts re-
search in the field of cancer.

Frania with Pola and Sam during her visit to the
United States.

Chapter 14
Frania Comes to the United States

We remained in constant touch with Frania after we came to the United States. When the children were in elementary school, we invited her to visit us. She was very happy to come, but she was afraid we would not recognize her. She visited Irene in New Jersey first and stayed there six weeks. Then she came here and we immediately recognized each other. I was overjoyed to see her after so many years. When she saw me she smiled and we kissed and hugged each other. We brought her home and she played with my children the same way she played with us: making cookies with Sherry and washing Jack's hair. The children adored her.

Our roles had reversed. I served Frania breakfast in bed and we had a terrific time. When the children went to summer camp, Frania went with us. After we left the children at camp, we gave Frania a little tour of the United States. I don't think she

Pola and Frania in Atlanta.

told anyone in Poland that she had helped us and that she was visiting Jews in the United States. We asked her to stay in the United States with us but Frania declined because she couldn't speak English and we lived in the suburbs. In Poland, she lived in the city where she could walk to church every day and do her shopping and meet her friends. She didn't have to work because we willingly supported her.

Frania stayed with us for six weeks and then we took her to the airport. Before she left us, I gave her some money and we put it in her shoe. At the plane, they allowed me to go aboard with her and we sat together and cried. She told me that she would never see me again.

A year later Frania passed away. She became ill a few months after she returned with cancer of the

Frania's last letter to Pola. She dictated it to her niece, Genia. The letter relates that Frania is very ill.

Genowefa Badecka
59-220 Legnica
ul. Złotoryjska 35/4

Frania

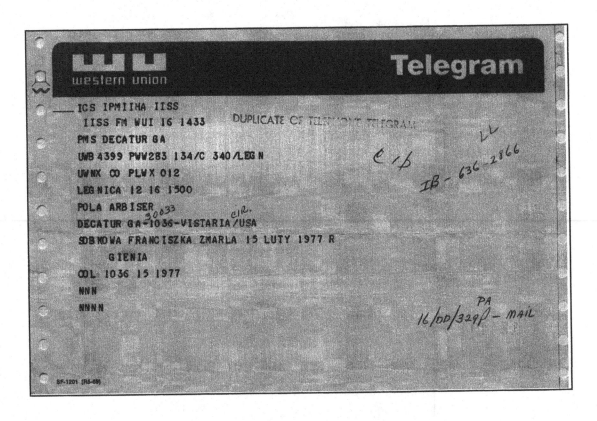

The telegram sent by Genia to the Arbisers informing them
that Frania had died on February 15, 1977.

Frania's funeral.

liver. We sent money for her hospital bills and medication. Her niece sent us a letter and a picture of her funeral. Frania is in our heart forever. We still correspond with and send pictures to her family and take care of her niece. A few months ago, my sister Irene went to Poland and met Frania's niece for the first time.

My younger sister, Irene, also came to the United States a few months after our arrival. She stayed for awhile with us in Atlanta and then decided to go to New York. There she met her future husband, Eugene Frisch. Eugene came from the city of Kolomya. Like Sam, he had survived the war in Russia. After liberation he returned to Poland to find that no one in his family had survived. He went to Italy where he attended university and got a Ph.D. in civil engineering. Then he came to New York. My sister and Eugene met and after a short courtship they were married and had two children.

Irene came to the United States after two years of medical school in Heidelberg, Germany. Soon after the birth of her children Irene was accepted at Columbia University, School of Library Science

Irene and Eugene Frisch's wedding picture.

where she got her Masters Degree. She became a medical librarian and had a long and successful career.

Meantime, her children finished school and went to college. Benjamin (Randy), her son, finished Wesleyan University and went to California to become a musician. Later, he finished his education at the Boston University Law School. He now owns and operates a music publishing company in New York City. Sharone, her daughter, studied at University of Pennsylvania and later attended George Washington University Law School. She divides her time between practicing law and being a wife to Paul Kornman and the mother of three children: Isabel, Jacob, and Joseph.

After my sister and her husband retired, they sold their house in Teaneck, New Jersey and moved to Fort Lee, New Jersey where they live in a high rise. Today, they are enjoying the success of their children.

While Irene lived in Teaneck she wrote many articles for a local newspapers which were nicely received. For *Mother's Day* she wrote an article called "Almost A Mother" about Frania for which she won a prize. Some of her articles were published in *Chicken Soup for the Jewish Soul*.

ALMOST A MOTHER

Although my own mother has been dead for a long time, I remember her vividly, always with great love. Yet on this Mother's Day I am thinking about a woman who never had children of her own, a woman who touched my life with her strong and loving hand, a woman who risked her own life to save mine.

Our story began 65 years ago in our little city in Poland. My mother, a young housewife at the time, took her baby son for a walk in his stroller. Little did she know at the time that this would be the most important walk of her life. On her way to the park she was stopped by a teenaged peasant girl. "What a beautiful baby," the girl exclaimed. "Can I play with him?"

This was music to the ears of a young mother, who adored her chubby firstborn. "Surely," she responded. "And what is your name, and where are you from?" The girl was about 15 years old, blonde, with two long braids, smiling blue eyes, and a perky nose. She was barefoot, her only pair of shoes tied together and hung over her shoulder (as shoes were to be saved and not worn.) In her hand she carried a colorful kerchief tied into a bundle, containing all of her possessions.

"My name is Frania," the girl replied. She had come to the city looking for a job in a household. While she spoke with my mother, she shook the rattle, made faces and cooed at the baby. It was obvious that she was quite smitten. My mother, who was generally not one to make hasty decisions, somehow made up her mind at that very instant.

"You have found a job right now," she said, and took the girl home with her. This was a time when hiring people was less complex than today. People trusted each other and small town life was easy, with no media to frighten anyone with reports of outrageous crimes. And so Frania became a member of our household.

Frania's father had died when she was five. Her mother, a poor farmer and widow, was left with little land and many children. The children had all started working at an early age. Frania started her first job at age six, tending the geese of a wealthy farmer. Although her formal education ended at this point, she never ceased to learn. She was observant and gifted with both natural intelligence and a great deal of common sense. Although she was illiterate, she developed into a capable young woman who was well-equipped to deal with any situation she found herself in.

Frania was part of our household for 14 years, witnessing the arrival of my sister and then me. All that time she was extremely devoted to us and remained convinced that "our children" were the smartest and the most special. A devout Catholic, she instilled in us her faith and fear of G-d. In her own simple way, she taught us right and wrong. Her values were high and her code of ethics strong, supported by tales of her youth and by examples from village life. She gave us all the security in the world and would have easily won the approval of today's child psychologists.

During World War II she did not hesitate for one moment to save our lives, although it meant endangering her own, devising the most outlandish tactics in order to outsmart our persecutors. Many years later, already old, she was reluctant to accept our help, afraid that she might deprive us of something.

Today, dear Frania, I hope that you are in your much coveted and deserved paradise. I hope as you read this tribute, you are happily sharing it with your neighbors and saying "our children did it again," as proud of me now as you always were.

Irene Frisch

Chapter 15
Witness

Since my retirement, my life has changed—it is not
as structured as it was before. Now that I have some
free time on my hands, I decided to devote my time
to volunteering at the William Breman Jewish Heritage Museum in Atlanta, Georgia. At the Museum I
speak to groups of young adults who have come to
tour the Holocaust Gallery and sometimes I talk at
churches, synagogues, and schools. When I tell them
about the survival of my mother, sister, and myself
during the Holocaust, the hero of my account is
Frania, the savior of my family. It is very important to me to tell as many people as I can what one
person can do, even at the risk to her own life, to
save other lives without any material reward.

As I get older and have more time to reminisce, I
realize what a tremendous deed Frania did. She not
only saved my mother, sister and myself, but generations to come. Thanks to her, we have children and

The dedication of the Arbiser Family Theater at the
William Breman Jewish Heritage Museum in 1999.

The William Breman Jewish Heritage Museum
would be pleased to have you join us as we honor
Sam and Pola Bienstock Arbiser
upon the dedication of
The Arbiser Family Theater
and the presentation by
the Government of Israel on behalf of Yad Vashem, Jerusalem,
naming Franciszka Sobkowa, rescuer of the Bienstock family,
'among the righteous'

Sunday, July 11, 1999
3:00 p.m.
The William Breman Jewish Heritage Museum
1440 Spring Street, NW
Atlanta, Georgia 30309

Hosted by
Zoya and Jack Arbiser 404-486-9411
Sherry and Lee Bagel 770-698-0366

Reception to follow

192

grandchildren. No one can give more than risking their life to save others.

At the William Breman Jewish Heritage Museum pictures of Frania and my family are featured in the Holocaust Gallery. The theater in which I speak carries the name of the Arbiser family. On exhibit near the door of the theater is a medal and certificate from Yad Vashem in Israel honoring Frania as a "Righteous Gentile" for risking her life and in the process saving generations to come. Yad Vashem is very strict about the criteria for a "righteous gentile." One of the conditions is that the rescuer must not have accepted money in exchange for their help. It took many years, but I finally received a medal and Certificate of Honor formally designating Frania as a "Righteous Gentile." She is also listed on the 'Plaque of Honor' and has a tree in the 'Garden of Righteous Gentiles' at Yad Vashem in Jerusalem. The medal and Certificate of Honor are on display where the visitors, including many children, can see and appreciate her selfless sacrifices.

IRENE'S VISIT TO POLAND

Visiting Drohobycz and realizing my second dream was not so easy. Several years ago, I traveled to Europe and stopped in Poland. I stood in line at the Russian Consulate's office, hoping to gain a visa to visit Drohobycz. When my efforts failed, I left, disappointed.

Last year, in 2000, Genia invited me to her daughter's wedding. How time flies! I still remembered Genia's father, Frania's brother, as a dashing young soldier in 1939. Without thinking, I quickly wrote to congratulate Genia and to accept her invitation. I had an ulterior motive: The wedding would take place in Poland, not far from Drohobycz. Since Drohobycz now belonged to the Ukraine and unrestricted travel was possible, I saw before me an opportunity to visit my hometown.

I was excited, but also scared to return to Drohobycz. I remembered the Gentiles' cruelty and witnessed their hateful actions toward the Jews. And so, I asked that Genia or her husband accompany me on my visit to Drohobycz. Genia's next letter included detailed plans for the wedding, photographs of the young couple and both sets of parents, and her promise that she or her husband would take me to Drohobycz.

The next morning I stood in line at the Ukrainian Consulate's office hoping to obtain a visa. I was surrounded by an assortment of people: there were Poles, Russians, Ukrainians who wished to visit their families, and there were Chasidic Jews who wished to visit the graves of important rabbis. The clerk who asked me the reason for my visit to Drohobycz was puzzled by my answer. I could not provide the name of any person I wish to visit. When I explained I had sentimental reasons, he repeated my story to a co-worker. They both stared at me as if I were crazy. Nonetheless, they accepted my visa application and sent me home to wait for my papers.

My passport and visa arrived two weeks later. My husband, after years of insisting he had no wish to travel to Poland (he is also from Poland and also survived the war under horrific circumstances), suddenly decided to join me on the trip. He planned to attend the wedding and then tour Warsaw. But, he would not travel to Drohobycz. He had lost a large family during the war and claimed that going back would break his heart. We made hotel reservations in Warsaw, purchased plane tickets, packed gifts for our hosts, and awaited our date of departure.

Our first stop was in Warsaw—Varsovia—the capital city of Poland. The last time I was in Warsaw was 1949, just before my family moved to Israel. The city had been bombed and destroyed. One could walk for miles without seeing an intact building. Now, we looked out upon a beautiful, rebuilt city. As we toured the city, I recalled the exciting stories my parents had told me after each visit to Warsaw before the war, and the many stories I had read about Jewish artists and writers from Warsaw.

One day, while my husband and I strolled through the city, we spotted a man selling small, hand-carved wooden figurines. He was the proud artist. Physically, he was ugly. He had a fat nose, rheumy eyes, a crooked mouth, a hunchback, and legs and arms that appeared twisted by arthritis or some other illness. As we approached his stand, we saw that his collection consisted of ugly caricatures of Jewish characters: a shoemaker, a baker, a tailor, and so on, all displaying long hooked noses, oversized ears, and large out-stretched greedy hands. This was exactly how the Germans had depicted the Jews in their propaganda paper, *Der Sturmer*.

I purchased a figurine of an ugly Jew holding a bag on which was printed a dollar sign. I then asked the man: "Where can one see a Jew like this?" I then added: "Look at my husband, he is Jewish." My husband is blond, blue-eyed, and has handsome classic features. In fact, he is the 'Aryan' prototype. The artist, without blinking an eye, answered: "Some Jews gave their family pictures to my parents to hide during the war, and never returned to claim them. I have looked at the pictures and this is how I saw the people." I saw no point in arguing.

After Warsaw, we boarded a train to our next destination, the wedding in Legnica. Genia's husband,

Peter, greeted us at the train station and took us directly to the church. I immediately recognized Genia. Genia and Peter were an attractive, nice couple with two beautiful daughters. They gave us a royal reception, including us in the wedding preparations and inviting us to numerous events. The ceremony took place in an old, beautiful church not far from where I completed high school in 1949.

After the ceremony, a caravan of cars left for a small town in the mountains. We took over an entire hotel for two days. No expense was spared. Guests celebrated late into the night and awoke, the next morning, to the smell of pigs roasting, the sound of vodka flowing, and a sunny day. Music played non-stop for two days. Although Genia (and probably some others) knew of my connection to Frania and the circumstances of my survival during the war, that subject—in fact, the entire war—never came up during our entire visit.

After the wedding, I began making preparations for my visit to Drohobycz. Genia's husband, Peter, and I would travel first by train, then by bus. I traveled lightly, removing my jewelry and attempting to blend in with the local crowd. We arrived in Drohobycz the second day of our trip, at about noon. After checking in at our hotel, which was shabby and dirty, and freshening up, we hailed a taxi and headed for my childhood home.

The taxi stopped in front of a house, only it did not look like my family's home. This house was painted a dark shade; our little garden was gone, replaced by weeds; our red fence was missing; our beautiful entrance was replaced with an ugly, plain door. When I went around to the back of this building, I saw two more doors, one with a terrace. The doors and terrace were not part of my family's home. In short, this house was not recognizable to me.

An older man and a little boy, his grandson, came out of the house. I told them in Ukrainian, that I had lived in this house as a child and would like to enter. He informed me that he had purchased the house from the city and now lived there with his family. He was polite and admitted Peter and me into the house.

I saw the house was now subdivided into three apartments. The beautiful grand entrance hall that my father had been so proud of was now gone. Each room appeared different than the rooms in my memory. I entered the room where my brother, Ludwik, had died more than sixty years before. I was bewildered at my detachment, at the fact that I felt nothing.

As I walked from room to room, I continued to feel nothing. I walked out of the house. The taxi was still standing in front of the house and a small group of people waited outside. It is not everyday that a taxi appears on Zupna Street. Peter was talking to the neighbors, probably telling them my story. For me it was like a dream. I do not believe that I was functioning properly. I inquired about old-time neighbors—there was no one. The Russians have a way of relocating people and all the inhabitants came from different parts of the Ukraine in the 1950s.

At one time, many years ago there was a large courtyard with several houses. It all belonged to my grandfather, who lived in one multi-family house and I was born there. There was once a large well-kept garden, now overflowing with weeds. The house where I was born and lived until I was about three years old was now delapidated.

It was already afternoon. I had not eaten for about twenty hours and Peter and I inquired about a place to eat. The driver took us to a restaurant two or three blocks away. It was once an apartment house of two or three stories and was quite large for a small town. My father had friends there and spent many afternoons in a beautiful garden playing cards in a gazebo. I used to accompany him. The place was very familiar to me. Now only one sidewall was standing although it still had balconies. I do not understand how the wall was supported or what had happened to the rest of the building. Now there was a long hall attached with a terrace and it housed a restaurant that was very unusual and primitive.

After lunch we toured the city. Although more than half a century had passed since I had left, I found that I still knew the city by heart. I am known for my proverbial luck of orientation. Here I found places where we used to live: my school, my father's store, and finally—without any hesitation—the building were Frania lived and where we had hidden.

I went there at night. We left at night as Frania did not want her neighbors to know she was saving Jews. Somehow guided by a supernatural force, I found the house. It was not centrally located. I looked at the window, where for a long time I stood behind a curtain looking outside envying the rabbits, cats, and dogs their freedom. One of Frania's neighbors, an old maid at the time had a habit of shaking out every part of her wardrobe, including her underwear and shoes. As we had nothing else to do we observed from behind the curtain the habits of the neighbors. Secretly, we gave the woman the nickname "The Shaker." As I stood in front of the house, a window—the same window—opened and a hand with a white rug appeared and shook it out.

After this we drove to the outskirts of the town to the small forest where the Germans executed and buried many Jews. The place is called Bronica. My cousin one year older than I, who had the same first and last name, was killed and buried here with her mother. She was a lovely child of about eleven or twelve years of age at the time of her death. Many of my friends and neighbors were buried there as well. I said a silent prayer for them.

About six years ago, survivors from my hometown made a pilgrimage there. They came from different parts of the world. Each of them had someone dear buried there and they put up a large monument. The mayor of the town gave a beautiful speech, a film was made, and I got a copy. Now the monument was desecrated, torn and filled with garbage. I was heartbroken. I did not want to linger anymore in Drohobycz. We hired another taxi and went back to Przemysl, at the Polish border.

* * * * *

During World War II, I witnessed and experienced many of the atrocities that came to be called the

"Holocaust": the murder of people dear to me, the cruelty of German soldiers, and the betrayal by good friends and neighbors. However, I also witnessed and experienced the kindness of a simple, uneducated woman who risked her life in order to save mine. Frania was a member of our household for fourteen years. She was devoted to us and was convinced that we—her substitute children—were the smartest and the most special. A devout Catholic, she instilled in us her faith and fear of G-d despite the fact that we did not share her precise faith. In her own simple way, she taught us right from wrong. Her values were high and her ethics strong, supported by tales of her youth, and more importantly, demonstrated by her selfless acts during the war.

The shelves of American libraries and bookstores are filled with book, movies, and articles about the Holocaust. There is no need for one more story of survival. Yet, the story of Frania—the simple, Catholic woman who saved our lives while risking her own—has not been written. Without this book, her story would surely be forgotten. Therefore, I

continue to admire Pola for the wisdom and forti-
tude she has shown during our pre-war years, our
years in hiding, our years following the war, and
her current persistence in telling Frania's story
in this book.
Irene Frisch

Sam in Siberia during the war

SAM ARBISER'S STORY

"In your life, you may never see a real hero. But, you see that lady sitting there—she is a hero." These words were said by my cousin, Martin, to his 11-year-old son. He pointed to an ordinary woman of small build in her seventies with grey hair who was sitting on the sofa, speaking Polish with my wife. Her name was Frania Sobkowa. My wife, Pola, and her sister, Irene, are both here today because of Frania.

It took an immense amount of work to overcome the Communist Polish bureaucracy, but Irene and Pola were both determined to bring Frania to the United States. Frania flew to New York and spent the first six weeks of her visit to the United States with Irene and her family in Teaneck, New Jersey. Then she came to Atlanta to visit our family. Pola and I, in a high state of excitement, were waiting for her at the airport. Finally, after most of the people had gotten off the plane she appeared. After hugging, kissing, and many tears Pola introduced me to Frania. It was a great moment in my life.

But, in many ways, I felt that I already knew Frania from the multiple letters and pictures that had been sent back and forth between the United States and Poland for many years. The Bienstocks, as a family, were in continuous contact with Frania and together made it possible for Frania to have a very comfortable life in Poland.

Frania was overwhelmed by the United States. It was an entirely different world. Everything was open, available, with no long lines. There was the noise of traffic and, of course, the malls.

The summer of Frania's visit, our children, Jack and Sherry, were at the Blue Star summer camp in Hendersonville, North Carolina. When we went to pick them up we brought Frania with us. The children and Frania became instant friends.

In the evenings we sat with Frania and reminisced about the times—both good and bad—during their time in Poland and our miraculous survival. It was very hard for both Pola and Frania to separate again—this time probably forever.

I grew up in a middle-class family: my father, Jacob, was a Zionist; Pola, my beautiful mother; Nathan, a younger brother who also later fled Warsaw; Hela, my sister; and Israel, another brother. All perished in the Holocaust except Nathan and myself.

When I decided to escape from Warsaw in the weeks after Poland fell to the Germans, my mother, who did not look Jewish, bravely accompanied me to the border of Russian-occupied Poland. Many lost their lives attempting to do the same. The route from Warsaw to the River Bug which separated the German- and Russian-occupied parts of Poland was very dangerous. At any moment, a Pole could point and call a German SS man and say: "Look, a Jew!" What followed invariably finished tragically.

Sam's family about 1942: His mother (who was also named Pola) is on the left; his father, Jacob is on the right and his brother and sister, Israel and Hela, are in the middle. All were murdered at Treblinka death camp.

Sam's mother, Pola Arbiser, and his sister, Hela, in the Warsaw ghetto.

Sam's father, Jacob Arbiser, in 1918

My mother and I separated at the border. I was never to see her again. Before me was the River Bug which I had to cross. Because I had only a few *zlotys* in my pocket I could not afford to rent a boat from a local fisherman. However, I knew blacksmithing—a trade I learned at my grandfather's foundry during vacations—and I worked for two days for a fisherman who lived near the river. In exchange, one early morning he transferred me across the river to the Russian side with directions on how to reach the city of Brest.

I thanked him and was following his directions when two Russian cavalry-men captured me. They took me to the fortress in Brest from which, in the first of many miracles to come, I was able to sneak out. I ran to the railway station and boarded a train for Bialystok without a penny and no ticket. I made it by desperately avoiding the conductor for the entire journey.

Bialystok was overcrowded with Jewish refugees and there was no place to sleep, no food, and plenty of lice. I got a job repairing locomotives. Some days later my brother, Nathan, who had almost been shot by the Russians in his flight from Warsaw, arrived in Bialystok as well. I left Bialystok with my brother and other friends from Warsaw who had also arrived. We went to Krasnoyarsk in Siberia.

After four weeks in a cattle car we arrived in Siberia where bread and soap were hard to get. Nathan and I were lucky to be assigned to a machine shop. Machine building was and is our family tradition and has been the main source of income for several generations. In addition, the director of the local evening high school, Sophia Natanovna, visited our dormitory and enrolled us in an evening high school which we attended after our workday was done.

I received a warm reception from my fellow students. Nadiezda, was the sister of the school's director. In a way, she was also a kind of Frania. She took me aside after we had been in school for several months and said: "I'm risking my life telling you this but you must stop talking about politics." We had been complaining bitterly about the lack of basic things. She told me that in every dormitory there were NKVD (the name of the Soviet espionage organization before it became the KGB) snitches. I told my brother and my best friend, Tadek. We all followed her advice. Two other men may have run afoul of these snitches in some way—one morning they were missing from our dormitory. We never found out what happened to them. I also met in Russia a pretty medical student whose name was Marinka. Her father was very nice to me, he sometimes gave me illegal ration coupons for bread. In another incident she also saved myself and my brother from the hands of of the NKVD. She now lives in the United States with her husband and family.

In early 1941, from the windows of our dormitory we saw Russian trains begin rolling from east to west day and night loaded with tanks and air-planes. It was obvious that there was going to be a war between Germany and Russia. Nathan and I were mobilized just one week before the out-break of the war with Germany in June 1941. We were placed together into working units with the worst elements of Soviet society. While I was in the Russian *Stroy Bat* (Building Battalions), I loaded boulders into trucks from a quarry near the River Tom. When they blasted the stone in the quarry, it was our job to retrieve those pieces of stone that had fallen into the river.

Then another miracle occurred. I was rescued from the murderous work of lifting rocks from the river by a Jewish "*nachalnik*" (boss) who assigned Nathan and me to manage the meager library. Was he a kind of Frania? Undoubtedly he did save both our lives but, unlike Frania, he didn't risk his own life. Working in the library enabled Nathan and me to continue our education and after four very hungry years we both got a masters degree in mechanical engineering.

When I said goodbye to the Director of the Institute, who was a devoted Communist, and shook his hand, he said to me in clear Hebrew: "*Beshana habaa b'Yerushalim.*" ("Next year in Jerusalem.") I was pleasantly shocked.

In this way the years went by in Russia. One day I read in *Pravda* (a Russian newspaper) just one sentence: "The Americans have dropped an atomic bomb on Japan." Soon the war finished, after many celebrations my brother, his wife, and myself started thinking about returning to Poland and to our family. Luckily, the Soviets and new pro-communist government of Poland agreed that ex-Polish citizens could return to Poland.

The journey from Siberia back to Poland was very long and arduous. Finally, after five weeks of riding in cattle cars we arrived in the completely bombed-out city of Warsaw. When we returned to our family home on Mila Street we found that the entire area had been totally devastated. No buildings stood there. This was not surprising since it was on Mila Street that the Jewish resistance fighters of the ghetto made their stand during the Warsaw Ghetto Uprising in April 1943. My parents, brother, and sister were gone. Later, a survivor told me he had seen them being loaded onto a train and that they had been taken to the Treblinka death camp where they were murdered.

The next four years in Poland under Communist rule were uneventful. Some of the events were pleasant, but mostly we spent our time trying to avoid the UB (Polish Secret Police) and our antisemitic Polish neighbors. I decided to leave Poland and immigrate to Israel.

In January 1950 Nathan and I landed in Haifa and were initially put into a DP camp along with the other new arrivals. As soon as I could, I took a bus to Vulcan, the largest foundry in Israel where I got a job and started over again from the beginning. I didn't even have the fare to get back to the camp from the foundry and had to borrow it from the director who interviewed and hired me.

In Haifa I had made few friends as I was mostly absorbed in my work, mechanical engineering. I climbed the ladder nicely and after three years I became the head of the machine building department in the largest machine building foundry in the Middle East.

As any young man in Israel I had to join the army. I was a member of a commando unit where they said: "You only make a mistake once in your life." Some time later I met a beautiful, smart, and intelligent girl. Her name was

214

Above: Sam in front of the ruins of his high school on Grzybowska Street in Warsaw (later in the Warsaw ghetto area) after the war.

Right: Sam in front of the ruins of his home on Mila Street in Warsaw (later in the Warsaw ghetto area) after the war.

Pola and one year later we married in a small ceremony attended by Pola's father and mother, my Aunt Frieda, my brother Nathan and his wife, and a few good friends. Since I still lived in Haifa because of my work and Pola was a student at the Hebrew University in Jerusalem, we met once a week in Tel Aviv. Eventually I got a position closer to Tel Aviv.

From Pola I first learned about Frania, the woman who had saved her life during the war, and who was always in her thoughts. Both Pola and I and Frania wrote to each other continuously and we supported her and made it possible for Frania to live comfortably.

Then I got an offer from an American company to come to Chicago and work for them. I was ready to go but Pola was heartbroken, although she agreed to go. Nathan and his wife, Frieda, who were married in Siberia, took us to the ship and we departed for the United State via Europe.

We landed in New York in December 1959 and were picked up by relatives from my father's side of the family. I went to Chicago and Pola went to Atlanta with them. I eventually ended up in Atlanta as well where I landed a job in a machine building company.

Our children, now grown with families of their own, heard about Frania daily from the many stories told by Pola. For them, Frania's visit to Atlanta was very special. Years have passed since her visit and Frania has since died, but though Pola and myself reminisce about our parents very often—there is no day without Frania.

Frania's Legacy: The Arbiser and Frisch Families

The Arbiser family:
Front row seated: Jordan Bagel, Pola Arbiser (holding Marlee Bagel), Ilan Arbiser (child), Adam (held by Zoya) and Ethan Arbiser (held by Jack)
Back row standing: Sherry Bagel, Sam Arbiser and Lee Bagel (Sherry's husband)

Above: Sherry Bagel, Sam and Pola Arbiser, Mr. and Mrs. Patillo, Jack and Zoya Arbiser

Above: Sam and Pola Arbiser, Nathan Arbiser (Sam's brother), Irene Frisch (sitting front), and Frieda Arbiser (Nathan's wife).

Pola Arbiser resides in Atlanta, Georgia with her husband, Sam, and two married children and grandchildren. Irene Frisch resides with her husband, Eugene, in Fort Lee, New Jersey. Their son, Benjamin (Randy) resides in New York and their daughter, Sharone, with her husband and children in Connecticut.

Pola speaks often at the William Breman Jewish Heritage Musuem to school children and adults about her experiences during the war and her family's savior, Franciszka Sobkowa.

In 1999, the Arbiser's endowed the Arbiser Family Theater at the Museum, which is dedicated to Frania, who has been honored as a Righteous Gentile by Yad Vashem in Jerusalem. A medal and certificate in her name adorn the wall outside the theater.

The extended Arbiser and Frisch families are alive today because of the courage and selflessness of one simple Polish woman, who understood the true meaning of Christian charity and kindness. Their journey from hiding during the war, from Europe to Israel and then to the United States was made possible by one woman—who proved that one good person can change the world.

I would like to thank my husband, Sam, for his patience and support during the writing of this book. - Pola Arbiser

---

Jack Arbiser (Pola and Sam's son) and his family. Jack, Zoya, Adam (being held by Zoya), and Ethan Arbiser. Not shown is their newest child, Joseph, born in 2001.

JACK ARBISER
(Pola and Sam's son)

It is a common saying that acts of kindness create ripples, similar to that of a pebble thrown in the water. Similarly, the kindness of Franciszka Sobkowa has rippled throughout the generations. The generation of my mother, my generation, and the generation of our children wouldn't have existed without her.

Our sages tell us that during the Passover *seder* (dinner), we should all consider that we personally were present at the Exodus from Egypt. This is an appropriate rule, because we owe our existence to an event beyond our control that occurred a generation before we were born. Similarly, our sages tell us that we must recount every year the story of our own redemption from Egypt. The goal of Egyptian slavery was to force us to lose our identity, while the goal of the Nazis was the physical extermination of the Jewish people. In both cases, we owe our redemption to Divine Intervention, not to our own strength and intelligence.

The story of my mother's upbringing has helped us put things in perspective. Whenever my sister or I had some problems in school and we complained, my mother would ask us two questions: (1) Are they shooting at you? (2) Are your classes being conducted in English? The answers to these questions was obvious and made us realize in retrospect that our problems are not so difficult. As long as you are healthy, virtually all problems have a solution. My mother's wartime experiences, along with her ten

221

years in Israel after the war, have helped instill a healthy self-confidence about her Jewish identity.

Her lifetime experiences have instilled the conviction that antisemites hate Jews not because of their behavior or actions, but because they exist. Again, this is a lesson described many centuries ago. When the Roman emperor Hadrian visited Jerusalem, a Jew saluted him. Hadrian said, "How dare a Jew salute me, off with his head." News of this action spread, and later that day, Hadrian passed in a parade, and a Jew did not salute him. Hadrian was angered and said, "How dare a Jew not salute me, off with his head." This lesson from Hadrian is also the lesson from Hitler. It is not Jewish behavior, whether it be assimilation or public religious observance that angers the antisemites, it is the fact that Jews exist, which provokes the antisemite. Thus concession or 'blame the victim' behavior will not yield any benefit.

From my mother's story, we have also learned that it is impossible to predict who will be your friend in times of trouble. Humans possess an endless capacity to rationalize their behaviors. Entire nations absolved themselves of responsibility during the Holocaust, citing that it was an internal German problem, or that the Jews brought the Holocaust on themselves. The actions of Franciszka Sobkowa, a decent individual who was able to save an entire family, surpassed the humanitarian actions of many nations during World War II. The purpose of this book is to illustrate the power of a single individual to bring good to the world.

SHERRY BAGEL
(Pola and Sam's daughter)

Sherry and Lee Bagel and their children, Ilan (being held), Marlee (seated front), Jordan, standing. Not shown is Zoe who was born in 2000.

Throughout my early childhood, I have heard stories about my mother's survival during the war and the key figure responsible for her survival, Frania.

I was not fortunate enough to meet my grandmothers. My father's entire family perished in the Warsaw ghetto and my maternal grandmother passed away after the war at an early age. Her name was Sara and I was named after both of my grandmothers, Sara and Yeffiay—which when translated means Sherry June.

The only grandparent that I was lucky enough to meet was my grandfather. He survived many concentration camps, including Auschwitz. He had a number on his arm. We had a special relationship and he passed away when I was ten.

When Frania came to visit, I was very young. I could not imagine that my mother would recognize her. My mother assured me that she would always

223

remember Frania's face. When they saw each other at the airport, I re-member seeing tears and hugs between these two women. We shared some special moments during her visit, similar to those I imagine a grand-daughter would have with a grandmother, among them cooking *pierogies* and other treats.

I felt that I knew Frania very well despite her short visit. She had been the subject of so many of my mother's childhood stories. Frania's visit was unforgettable. We are all here because of her. As a result of her kindness, two more generations of our family have continued. My young daughter was named in honor of Frania. I hope she will share some of the same qualities of her namesake, Frania.

The Frisch family: Eugene and Irene and their grandchildren (left to right): Isabel, Joseph, and Jacob.

EUGENE FRISCH
(Irene's husband)

I lost my entire family, including my younger brother, who was only 15, to the Holocaust. I miraculously survived by escaping to Russia, where I was drafted into a labor battalion and forced to dig trenches against advancing German tanks at Stalingrad. Being young and healthy, I survived the severe winters and starvation and returned to Poland after the war in 1945. Soon thereafter, I left illegally for Italy and settled in a displaced persons camp. I landed a job and resumed my studies in engineering, which I had begun in 1940 in Poland before the war. I graduated in 1951 with a doctorate in civil engineering and soon after emigrated to the United States, where I landed a job in New York City.

Irene arrived in America in 1960 and we met in New York in July, 1961. The heavens moved quickly to tie our destinies together. We shared similar backgrounds. We both grew up in southeastern Poland, spoke the same language, shared similar family customs, and had mutual feelings and outlooks as Holocaust survivors. We were married less than three months later on September 17, 1961.

Even before Frania came to visit us in New Jersey around 1974, I had heard so much about her from Irene that I felt I had known her for a long time. Frania's arrival in New York was very emotional, full of warm embraces and joyful tears. I was pleased that she approved of me as the "suitable" husband, perhaps destined by Providence to be the husband for Irene.

Irene.

To confirm the culinary legends circulating in our family, and to emphasize the approval of Irene's choice, Frania immediately suggested that she make *pierogi* the way we used to have in our youth.

A few days later, when Frania recovered from her jet lag and from the initial shock of arriving in America, we took her to Manhattan, where she was ovewhelmed by the high-rise buildings, the crowded sidewalks of Fifth Avenue, and the endless automobile traffic. Her impression of St. Patrick's Cathedral was that it was immense–both as to the size of the building and its many religious displays.

After Frania left our home to stay with Pola in Atlanta, we missed her very much. We remained in touch with her until her death, and have continued to correspond with her niece, Genia, in Legnica, Poland. In September 2000, we attended the wedding of Genia's daughter. Irene visited Frania's grave with flowers in her hand and love in her heart.

To this very day, the timeless proverbs that were part of the daily conversation in Frania's original village, and later in her life in Drohobycz and Legnica, have become an occasion for humorous, but practical, explanations and solutions to some of our daily dilemmas. Never place keys on the kitchen table. Never lay new purchases on a bed. When things are misplaced, turn over a drinking glass. Never go back if you forget to take something with you. We routinely apply these maxims. I must admit that even though I do not believe in them, I uphold them out of sentiment.

We never forget Frania for what she was and what heroic things she did to save the lives of Pola, Irene, and their mother. Whenever we are asked how we survived the Holocaust, the answer quickly turns to Frania's tiny apartment in Drohobycz, and Frania is wholeheartedly ascribed the title "Saint."

Irene Frisch with her daughter, Sharone (seated middle back), Sharone's husband, Paul Kornman and their daughter, Isabel.

Irene and Eugene Frisch and their son, (Benjamin) Randy (on the left)

BENJAMIN (RANDY) FRISCH
(Irene and Eugene's son)

Frania is a constant reminder to me of the 'righteous gentiles.' My mother always told us about Frania, even when we were little children. Years later, I am still awed by her bravery. She visited us in the United States when my sister and I were teenagers. She did not speak English, so we could not communicate. Yet she clearly loved my sister and me. Frania will always be remembered in our family. Growing up, I heard many stories about Frania helping our family survive. I am grateful that the whole story is now recorded in this book.

SHARONE KORNMAN
(Irene and Eugene's daughter)

A friend will sometimes ask if I can watch her child for a few hours. I think, "My house will be extra messy, our children may quarrel, I will have to stay home, and I may even have to prepare and extra meal." I usually say "yes" if it is convenient for me, if my children want this child to visit, or if the visit will be relatively short. But what if I had no children, or had just enough food for myself, of if the visit would last for several years?

When people ask how my mother survived the Holocaust, I tell them: "My mother, her sister, and their mother were hidden by the family nanny in a small, one-room apartment." It is a simple answer to give, but a difficult concept to accept.

We all know the story of the evils of the Holocaust, of the many people who helped to kill millions of innocents or who simply looked the other way while friends and neighbors were slaughtered. But there is another story about the Holocaust, the story of a few courageous people who risked everything to save those who were marked for death. I am proud to tell people the story of Frania, the noble woman who saved my mother and her family. I am proud that my aunt has chosen to publish this story.

APPENDIX

POLA'S POEMS

(translated into English)

POLA'S POEMS
WRITTEN WHILE SHE WAS IN HIDING

04 July 1943

STRENGTH MORNING EDITION

Fields of rye rustled
Through the whole world
Carried on their wings
The precious flower of a song.
    Do float, song, through the fields
    Carry on your wings
    Alleviation for the reapers
    Across the whole village.
And when the dusk envelops the field
And the night comes on,
You-on your wings-carry,
Song, a multitude of glorious sounds.

THOUGHTS ABOUT FREEDOM

05 July 1943

Oh my freedom, you longed-for one,
Let me come out to this God's world
With my eyes and soul, which are so thirsty,
Asking to finally look out from behind bars.
      So that I could come out and take in deeply
      The sun and the fields and this whole world
      And with my eyes wide open look around
      This world blooming like a mythical flower.
Alas, these are only my dreams,
Dreamed out in my distress and bondage
Which bring together various memories
And will ignite when the end of my misery comes.
      "Sylwester Ostrozny"

"Sylwester Ostrozny"
25 June 1943

RAIN

Silent street, veiled with mist of rain
One hears only monotonous tapping of the rain drops on the windowpanes,
Such silence as if before a storm
And the whole world is bored with these rains.

    Now and then wind moans softly
    As if it were giving up the world
    And then silence again or great silence
    And again wind and rain go hand-in-hand like brother with brother.

06 July 1943

NIGHT

Night full of charm flowed down over the earth
Starry and beautiful and intoxicating
Having some strange power within
Lifting various memories on its wings.

    It flowed down so softly with velvety steps
    Wrapping black fog around the whole God's world
    And flowing still farther along the blue trail
    Putting to sleep trees and each and every flower.

It is flowing so softly, holding everyone in its memory,
Listening to the gentle whispers of the brooks.
Then again it is allured by the song of
Chorus of nightingales singing in the grove.

    It is standing and looking, all ears,
    Before it turns around, the day is already creeping
    And with teary eye night looks longingly
    At its crumbling masterpiece.
        "Sylwester Ostrozny"

234